ITALIAN KEY WORDS

is a learning aid benefiting from computer analysis of 500,000 words. It consists of a list of the commonest two thousand words in Italian, with their meanings in English, arranged in decreasing order of frequency. The list is divided into a hundred units of twenty key words each, from which many more words may be derived. For masculine adjectives, feminine endings are given if irregular. For singular nouns, plurals are given if irregular. All the commonest irregular verbs are cited fully in the present indicative, with meanings, and the three regular conjugations are listed separately.

Gianpaolo Intronati has made sure that pupils in the first year of secondary school, or adult beginners, will be introduced to *all* the most frequently-occurring words in Italian within the first year of study. An English index allows the user to trace each word in the lists and indicates by its position in the book the relative frequency of that word. Some readers may not have realised that the commonest hundred words in Italian include only nine nouns: can you guess what they might be? The answer is given in the introduction to Gianpaolo Intronati's *Italian Key Words*. It is a companion volume to the standard Oleander *French Key Words* by Xavier-Yves Escande.

D1643358

ITALIAN
KEY WORDS

the basic 2,000-word vocabulary
arranged by frequency in a
hundred units

with comprehensive Italian and
English indexes

GIANPAOLO INTRONATI

The Oleander Press

The Oleander Press
17 Stansgate Avenue
Cambridge CB2 2QZ
England

The Oleander Press
80 Eighth Avenue, Suite 303
New York,
N.Y. 10011
U.S.A.

British Library Cataloguing in Publication Data
Intronati, Giovanni Paolo
   Italian key words. —(Oleander language and
   literature; v. 13)
   1. Italian language–Dictionaries–English
   2. English language–Dictionaries–Italian
   I. Title.

ISBN 0-906672-25-2

Printed in Great Britain by BPCC Wheatons Ltd, Exeter

CONTENTS

CONTENTS

Introduction

Italian Key Words has been designed as an efficient, logical, and practical computer-based word-list for anglophone learners of Italian in their first year. It has been based with the author's permission on Xavier-Yves Escande's *French Key Words* (Oleander). The basic two thousand 'key' words are so called because by learning these thoroughly one unlocks the door to several thousand more words: plurals from singulars, feminines from masculines, and parts of the present tense from an infinitive.

The purpose of this technique is to stimulate confidence in the learning of Italian by teaching the commonest words first, and leaving the less common till later. *Italian Key Words* is intended to be used with a conventional grammar, a conventional dictionary, and a sound aid such as a cassette or video to improve pronunciation. A massive dictionary has been found in practice to unnerve the beginner, while most available Italian readers introduce too early words or ideas which may be arbitrary or advanced. At this sensitive phase, where interest in learning Italian can be so easily encouraged or discouraged, it is suggested that the student should be asked to learn words in a hundred manageable units of about twenty 'key' words each, thus mastering two thousand such words by the end of the first year. Only then will the student be ready to absorb unusual words of low occurrence. Computer-based methods are by now fully entrenched in mathematics and the sciences, but statistical sampling has hitherto been rarely practised in language learning, probably because of the difficulty of creating a sufficiently large data base to make the frequency list reliable. *Italian Key Words* is an ideal revision aid for first-year examinations, because you realise that you *must* know all these words.

The Units

Each of the hundred units is deliberately self-contained for ease of mastery. Unit 1 contains the twenty commonest Italian words, Unit 2 the next twenty commonest and so on. The key word is followed by an indication of its part of speech: *adj.*, adjective, *adv.*, adverb; *conj.*, conjunction; *f.n.*, feminine noun; *m.n.* masculine noun; *prep.*, preposition; *pron.*, pronoun. Verbs are not so shown, because they are always represented by the infinitive, which is in every case translated by the commonest meanings beginning with 'to'.

Masculine nouns and adjectives form their feminine by changing *o* to *a* unless otherwise shown. So masculine *ricco* becomes *ricca*. Singular nouns and adjectives if masculine form their plural by changing *o* to *i* unless otherwise shown. So singular *povero* becomes plural *poveri*. Similarly, if feminine, singular nouns and adjectives form their plural by changing *a* to *e* unless otherwise shown. So singular *povera* becomes plural *povere*. *Lo stato povero* in the singular becomes *gli stati poveri* in the plural; and *la casa povera* becomes *le case povere*. (The change above in the article occurs because of the rule changing *il* to *lo* and *i* to *gli* before *gn, z*, and the so-called 'impure *s*', which refers to any *s* followed by a consonant, as in *lo sport*.)

Regular verbs are conjugated in the present tense in model form in a separate table. The commonest irregular verbs are conjugated in the present tense (of the active voice, indicative mood) wherever their infinitive occurs in the order of frequency. Though verbs appear only in their infinitive form, their position in the units is judged from the total occurrence of all their parts. Occasionally a phrase connected with a word, usually a verb, has been inserted where the phrase is particularly common or could not be constructed without special knowledge.

Homographs are shown as one word if multiple meanings share one part of speech (*volta*, time, vault), but as two or more words if they do not: (*lo, art.* meaning 'the' in Unit 1 but *lo, pron.* meaning 'him, it' in Unit 2).

Many Italian words may be translated by a number of English equivalents. It would be counter-productive, in a work designed to stimulate the interest rather than clog the memory, to list all such equivalents, so only the most common have been cited. When consulting the indexes, therefore, the reader should try to think of synonyms or near-synonyms if a given word appears not to be included.

The Indexes

Two indexes permit the reader to use *Italian Key Words* as a basic dictionary, but once again let it be stressed that the best available dictionary should be purchased if it is intended to continue with Italian past the elementary stage. Another fascinating use of the indexes is to discover how frequent – and consequently how relatively useful – each Italian word happens to be. Of course, the frequency level applies only to the *Italian* words: nothing is implied at any point about the relative frequency of the English equivalents. Even the most casual learner may be curious to learn that among the hundred most frequent words in Italian only nine are nouns: if you care to guess which they are now, you can compare your guesses with the answers, given at the end of this Introduction.

Apart from the indefinite and definite articles (un, uno, una; il, lo, la), if one counts the indefinite article also as a numeral, then only one other numeral (*due*) occurs among the commonest hundred words. Eleven are prepositions, eight conjunctions, twenty-three pronouns, eleven adverbs, fourteen adjectives, and nineteen verbs, including the auxiliaries andare, avere, essere and fare.

The Sources

The word-list has been based on a wide variety of sources, but primarily on Alphonse Juilland and others' *Frequency Dictionary of Italian Words* by kind permission of the publishers Mouton, The Hague. Adjustments in the order of frequency have been necessary to take into account later usage and the slightly different results obtained by other writers. All these writers have been motivated, as Juilland has stated, by "the importance of establishing a more standardised approach to vocabulary, in order to overcome the chaotic inconsistency of teaching materials chosen largely on subjective grounds".

M.E. Thompson's *Study in Italian Vocabulary Frequency* (Thesis, University of Iowa, 1927) established an objective vocabulary of 500 words for first-year students of Italian, with an alphabetical index of the words previously listed by frequency. The sample was drawn from 100,000 words used in ten Italian readers published in the U.S.A., but words were counted on only every tenth page of each book, reducing the sample's accuracy.

T.M. Knease produced a doctoral dissertation for the same university in 1931. Her *Italian Word List from Literary Sources* used a sample of 400,000 to produce a list of 2,000 words for more advanced students. The sample was drawn from forty authors listed in 'A Five Foot Shelf of Modern Italian Literature' (*Italica*, August 1925), covering books published between 1850 and 1930. Like Mary Thompson, Tacie Knease chose to eliminate a large number of high frequency words, vitiating her results, and counted words on intermediate pages only, in her case every fifth page.

L.H. Skinner produced a list of 3,000 words in 'A Comparative Study of the Vocabularies of Forty-Five Italian Textbooks' in *Modern Language Journal*, vol. XX, 1935. These grammars and readers were those in use in the U.S.A., but Laurence Skinner made the mistake of including words only in the vocabulary sections and omitting textual occurrences, so that *essere* appears in only 41 sources out of his 45, because four editors chose to omit the verb from their vocabulary, believing it to be too frequent to warrant insertion.

Bruno Migliorini, introducing *Der Grundlegende Wortschatz des Italienischen* (Marburg, 1943), gives no insight into how he arrived at his frequency list of the 1,500 commonest words.

Alphonse Juilland and Vincenzo Traversa provided the most serious undertaking of all, with their policy of equalizing subsamples in *Frequency Dictionary of Italian Words* (The Hague, 1973). Samples used were limited largely to those published between 1920 and 1940, and comprised a lexical universe of roughly half a million words divided into five equal subsamples of 100,000 words each drawn from plays, fiction, essays and memoirs, periodicals, and technical literature.

Frequency ratings assessed by Juilland have been followed quite closely, except that where his ratings differ significantly from those of his predecessors, a compromise has been reached, making the following lists probably even more accurate over the whole range of Italian than any preceding work.

Gianpaolo Intronati

N.B. The nine nouns occurring in the commonest hundred words are *anno, cosa, giorno, modo, parte, tempo, uomo, vita* and *volta*.

Regular Verbs in
The Present Tense

First Conjugation

Parlare, to speak

io parlo I speak
tu parli you (*s.*) speak
egli, essa parla he, she speaks

noi parliamo we speak
voi parlate you (*pl.*) speak
loro parlano they speak

Second Conjugation

Temere, to fear

io temo I fear
tu temi you fear
egli, essa teme he, she fears

noi temiamo we fear
voi temete you (*pl.*) fear
loro temono they fear

Third Conjugation (Group 1)

Sentire, to feel, listen

io sento I feel
tu senti you (*s.*) feel
egli, essa, sente he, she feels

noi sentiamo we feel
voi sentite you (*pl.*) feel
loro sentono they feel

Third Conjugation (Group 2)*

Capire, to understand

io capisco I understand
tu capisci you (*s.*) understand
egli, essa capisce he, she understands

noi capiamo we understand
voi capite you (*pl.*) understand
loro capiscono they understand

* Most 3rd conjugation verbs belong to this group, with the infix – isc – between stem and ending of the three singular persons and third person plural of the present, subjunctive, and imperative.

Unit 1

di *prep.* — of

il *art.* — the (*m.s.*)

la *art.* — the (*f.s..*)

e *conj.* — and

a *prep.* — to

in *prep.* — in

uno, una *art.* — a, an (*m., f.*)

essere — to be, being
- io sono I am — noi siamo we are
- tu sei you (*s.*) are — voi siete you (*pl.*) are
- egli è he is — loro sono they are

lo *art.* — the (*m.s.*), used instead of il before *gn*, impure *s* and *z*

che *pron.* — who, that

da *prep.* — from, by

per *prep.* — by, through

si *pron.* — one, -self

non *adv.* — not

con *prep.* — with

che *conj.* — than, that

avere — to have, having
- io ho I have — noi abbiamo we have
- tu hai you (*s.*) have — voi avete you (*pl.*) have
- egli ha he has — loro hanno they have

questo, questa *adj.* — this

Unit 2

ma *conj.* — but

su *prep.* — on

lo *pron.* — him, it

potere — to be able
- io posso I can — noi possiamo we can
- tu puoi you (*s.*) can — voi potete you (*pl.*) can
- egli può he can — loro possono they can

o *conj.* — or

anche *adv.* — also

fare — to do, make
- io faccio I do — noi facciamo we do
- tu fai you (*s.*) do — voi fate you (*pl.*) do
- egli fa he does — loro fanno they do

quello, quella *adj.* — that

suo, sua *adj.* — his, her(s), its

tutto, tutta *adj.* — every, all

come *adv.* — as, like

più *adv.* — more

dire — to say
- io dico I say — noi diciamo we say
- tu dici you (*s.*) say — voi dite you (*pl.*) say
- egli dice he says — loro dicono they say

dovere — to have to
- io devo I must — noi dobbiamo we must
- tu devi you (*s.*) must — voi dovete you must
- egli deve he must — loro devono they must

su *prep.* — on, upon

grande *adj.* — large, great

la *pron.* — her, it

Unit 3

stare | to stare, stand, etc.
    io sto I remain | noi stiamo we stop
    tu stai you (*s.*) wait | voi state you (*pl.*) live
    egli sta he stops | loro stanno they wait
ne *pron.* | some; of him, her, it (ne parlò con noi, he spoke of it with us)

quale *pron.* | which
due *num.* | two
venire | to come
    io vengo I come | noi veniamo we come
    tu vieni you (*s.*) come | voi venite you (*pl.*) come
    egli viene he comes | loro vengono they come
ci *pron.* | us, of it, to it (eccoci qua, here we are)

altro, altra *adj.* | other
più *m.n.* | the most
vedere | to see
    io vedo I see | noi vediamo we see
    tu vedi you (*s.*) see | voi vedete you (*pl.*) see
    egli vede he sees | loro vedono they see
quello, quella *pron.* | that one
ogni *adj.* | every, all
anno *m.n.* | year
perchè *conj.* | because, in order that
volere | to want, be willing.
    io voglio I wish | noi vogliamo we wish
    tu vuoi you (*s.*) wish | voi volete you (*pl.*) wish
    egli vuole he wishes | loro vogliono they wish
mio, mia *adj.* | my
senza *prep.* | without
loro *adj.* | their

Unit 4

sempre *adv.*	always, still
nostro *adj.*	our, ours
ancora *adv.*	still, yet
così *adv.*	thus, so
se *conj.*	if, whether
giorno *m.n.*	day
come *prep.*	as, like
primo *adj.*	first
poi *adv.*	then, after(wards)
cui *pron.*	whom, which
trovare	to find
quando *conj.*	when
andare	to go
io vado I go	noi andiamo we go
tu vai you go	voi andate you go
egli va he goes	loro vanno they go
sapere	to know
io so I know	noi sappiamo we know
tu sai you know	voi sapete you know
egli sa he knows	loro sanno they know
io *pron.*	I
uomo (*pl.* uomini) *m.n.*	man
già	already, formerly, indeed
cosa *f.n.*	thing
parte *f.n.*	part
volta *f.n.*	time, turn

Unit 5

ora *adv.*	now
tra *prep.*	between, among
fra *prep.*	within, among
altro *pron.*	other
qualche *adj.*	some, a few (with *sing.n. e.g.* qualche minuto, some minutes)
nuovo *adj.*	new
vita *f.n.*	life
mi *pron.*	me, to me
egli *pron.*	he
lui *pron.*	he, him
ora *f.n.*	hour, time
dove *adv.*	where
parlare	to speak
dopo *prep.*	after(wards)
noi *pron.*	we
tempo *m.n.*	time, weather
parere	to seem, look
io paio I appear	noi paiamo we appear
tu pari you appear	voi parete you appear
egli pare he appears	loro paiono they appear
modo *m.n.*	way, manner(s)
prendere	to take, catch
io prendo I take	noi prendiamo we take
tu prendi you take	voi prendete you take
egli prende he takes	loro prendono they take

Unit 6

passare	to pass
le *pron*.	to her, them
portare	to carry, wear
uno *pron*.	one
sè *pron*.	himself, herself, *etc*.
stesso *adj*.	same, self
pur(e) *adv*.	yet, likewise
questo, questa *pron*.	this one
sotto *prep*.	below, under
mettere	to put, place
io metto I put	noi mettiamo we put
tu metti you put	voi mettete you put
egli mette he puts	loro mettono they put
solamente *adv*.	only
li *pron*.	them
casa *f.n.*	house
bello *adj*.	handsome, beautiful
lasciare	to let, allow
forse *adv*.	perhaps
allora *adv*.	then
esso, essa *pron*.	he, she, it

Unit 7

parola *f.n.* — word
piccolo *adj.* — small
vero *adj.* — real, true
chi *pron.* — who(ever), whom
ti *pron.* — you (*s.*)
buono *adj.* — good
mai *adv.* — (n)ever
molto *adj.* — very, much
tenere — to keep, hold
    io tengo I keep   noi teniamo we keep
    tu tieni you keep   voi tenete you keep
    egli tiene he keeps   loro tengono they keep
solo *adj.* — alone, only
certo *adj.* — sure, certain
lavoro *m.n.* — work
tre *num.* — three
pensare — to think
poco *adj.* — little, few
sembrare — to seem, appear
ultimo *adj.* — last
bene *adv.* — well
alcuno *adj.* — no, any
rimanere — to remain
    io rimango I stay   noi rimaniamo we stay
    tu rimani you stay   voi rimanete you stay
    egli rimane he stays   loro rimangono they stay

Unit 8

donna *f.n.*	lady, woman
qui *adv.*	here
nome *m.n.*	name, noun
vi *pron.*	you, to you
contro *prep.*	against
alto *adj.*	high, tall
occhio *m.n.*	eye
oggi *adv.*	today
chiamare	to call, cry out
via *f.n.*	way, street
nè *conj.*	neither, nor
mano, la	hand
(*pl.* le mani) *f.n.*	
guardare	to look at, keep
mondo *m.n.*	world
proprio *adj.*	proper, neat
vecchio *adj.*	old
punto *m.n.*	point
città *f.n.*	city
ciò *pron.*	that, this, it
credere	to believe

Unit 9

momento *m.n.* — moment

prima *adv.* — before, earlier

terra *f.n.* — land, earth

tale *adj.* — such, like

subito *adv.* — suddenly

quasi *adv.* — almost, as if

tanto *adj.* — so much, such

verso *prep.* — towards

mentre *conj.* — while, whereas

fatto *m.n.* — fact, act(ion)

loro *pron.* — they

giungere — to arrive, reach

    io giungo I arrive   noi giungiamo we arrive

    tu giungi you arrive   voi giungete you arrive

    egli giunge he arrives   loro giungono they arrive

cercare — to seek, try

italiano *adj.* — Italian

nulla *adv.* — nothing

me *pron.* — me

padre *m.n.* — father

guerra *f.n.* — war

uscire — to leave, come out

    io esco I leave   noi usciamo we leave

    tu esci you leave   voi uscite you leave

    egli esce he leaves   loro escono they leave

mare *m.n.* — sea

Unit 10

conoscere — to know, be acquainted with
    io conosco I know — noi conosciamo we know
    tu conosci you know — voi conoscete you know
    egli conosce he knows — loro conoscono they know

però *conj.* — however, but
tornare — to return
acqua *f.n.* — water
entrare — to enter
forza *f.n.* — strength, power
notte *f.n.* — night
amore *m.n.* — love
figlio *m.n.* — son, boy
luce *f.n.* — light
cuore *m.n.* — heart
invece *adv.* — instead, on the contrary
caso *m.n.* — case, event

vivere — to live
    io vivo I live — noi viviamo we live
    tu vivi you live — voi vivete you live
    egli vive he lives — loro vivono they live

anzi *adv.* — rather, on the contrary
cominciare — to begin
là *adv.* — there

sentire — to feel, listen
    io sento I feel — noi sentiamo we feel
    tu senti you feel — voi sentite you feel
    egli sente he feels — loro sentono they feel

opera *f.n.* — work, opera

riuscire — to succeed
    io riesco I succeed — noi riusciamo we succeed
    tu riesci you succeed — voi riuscite you succeed
    egli riesce he succeeds — loro riescono they succeed

Unit 11

aria *f.n.* — air, breeze

lei *pron.* — she, her

seguire — to follow (conjugated like sentire)

sopra *prep.* — upon, above

gente *f.n.* — people

rendere — to give back, yield
- io rendo I give back
- tu rendi you give back
- egli rende he gives back
- noi rendiamo we give back
- voi rendete you give back
- loro rendono they give back

capo *m.n.* — head

apparire — to appear
- io appaio, apparisco I appear
- tu appari, apparisci you appear
- egli appare, apparisce he appears
- noi appariamo we appear
- voi apparite you appear
- loro appaiono, appariscono they appear

luogo *m.n.* — place

scrivere — to write
- io scrivo I write
- tu scrivi you write
- egli scrive he writes
- noi scriviamo we write
- voi scrivete you write
- loro scrivono they write

paese *m.n.* — land, town, village

presentare — to present

maggiore *adj.* — greater, larger

bisognare — to need, be necessary (bisogna scrivere, one must write)
- (3rd person sg. only)

continuare — to continue

aprire — to open
- io apro I open
- tu apri you open
- egli apre he opens
- noi apriamo we open
- voi aprite you open
- loro aprono they open

pensiero *m.n.* — thought

ordine *m.n.* — order, command

diventare — to become

idea *f.n.* — idea

Unit 12

riconoscere — to recognise (conjugated like conoscere)

fino *prep.* — until, as long as

servire — to serve (conjugated like sentire)

rappresentare — to represent, perform

intorno *prep.* — around

diverso *adj.* — different, various

chiedere — to ask

    io chiedo I ask   noi chiediamo we ask

    tu chiedi you ask   voi chiedete you ask

    egli chiede he asks   loro chiedono they ask

madre *f.n.* — mother

quattro *num.* — four

mese *m.n.* — month

popolo *m.n.* — people

cioè *adv.* — that is

anima *f.n.* — soul

pieno *adj.* — full

morte *f.n.* — death

secondo *adj.* — second, next

sera *f.n.* — evening

quindi *adv.* — therefore, afterwards

famiglia *f.n.* — family

Unit 13

voce *f.n.* — voice

restare — to stay, be left

fondo *m.n.* — end, background, bottom

morire — to die
- io muoio I die
- tu muori you die
- egli muore he dies

    noi moriamo we die
    voi morite you die
    loro muoiono they die

durante *prep.* — during

camera *f.n.* — room, chamber (*Eng.* camera is *It.* macchina fotografica)

correre — to run
- io corro I run
- tu corri you run
- egli corre he runs

    noi corriamo we run
    voi correte you run
    loro corrono they run

sole *m.n.* — sun

comprendere — to understand, include (conjugated like prendere)

nascere — to be born
- io nasco I am born
- tu nasci you are born
- egli nasce he is born

    noi nasciamo we are born
    voi nascete you are born
    loro nascono they are born

quale *adj.* — which, who

dunque *adv.* — so, then

trattare — to deal with, handle

presso *prep.* — near, by

corpo *m.n.* — body

arrivare — to arrive

ragione *f.n.* — reason, right (aver ragione, to be right)

vivo *adj.* — living

partire — to depart, set out (conjugated like sentire)

esistere — to exist
- io esisto I exist
- tu esisti you exist
- egli esiste he exists

    noi esistiamo we exist
    voi esistete you exist
    loro esistono they exist

Unit 14

antico *adj.* — ancient, old

condurre — to conduct, lead (*but Eng.* conduct (mus.) is It. dirigere)

io conduco I lead — noi conduciamo we lead
tu conduci you lead — voi conducete you lead
egli conduce he leads — loro conducono they lead

mostrare — to show

libro *m.n.* — book

professore *m.n.* — professor, teacher

chiudere — to close

io chiudo I close — noi chiudiamo we close
tu chiudi you close — voi chiudete you close
egli chiude he closes — loro chiudono they close

vario *adj.* — various, different

insieme *adv.* — together

persona *f.n.* — person

valore *m.n.* — value, courage

cielo *m.n.* — sky, heaven

campo *m.n.* — field, camp

stato *m.n.* — state

lungo *adj.* — long, tall

aspettare — to wait, expect

nessuno *pron.* — nobody, none

intendere — to mean, understand (conjugated like predere)

strada *f.n.* — street, way

finire — to finish (conjugated like capire)

chiaro *adj.* — clear, bright

Unit 15

salire — to climb, ascend
    io salgo — noi saliamo
    tu sali — voi salite
    egli sale — loro salgono
appena *adv*. — scarcely, as soon as
cadere — to fall, drop
    io cado — noi cadiamo
    tu cadi — voi cadete
    egli cade — loro cadono
carattere *n.m.* — character
possibile *adj.* — possible
perdere — to lose
    io perdo — noi perdiamo
    tu perdi — voi perdete
    egli perde — loro perdono
generale *adj.* — general
amico *m.n.* — friend
compiere — to complete
    io compio — noi compiamo
    tu compi — voi compite
    egli compie — loro compiono
figura *f.n.* — figure
spirito *m.n.* — spirit, wit
azione *f.n.* — action (but It. azione ordinaria in commerce is Eng. ordinary share)

lontano *adj.* — far, distant
umano *adj.* — human
no *adv.* — no

Unit 16

rispondere — to reply
    io rispondo — noi rispondiamo
    tu rispondi — voi rispondete
    egli risponde — loro rispondono

mancare — to lack, miss
    io manco — noi manchiamo
    tu manchi — voi mancate
    egli manca — loro mancano

signore *m.n.* — sir, Mr, gentleman

capire — to understand
    io capisco — noi capiamo
    tu capisci — voi capite
    egli capisce — loro capiscono

esempio *m.n.* — example

testa *f.n.* — head

ricco *adj.* — rich

ormai *adv.* — by now, henceforth

raggiungere — to achieve, reach
    io raggiungo — noi raggiungiamo
    tu raggiungi — voi raggiungete
    egli raggiunge — loro raggiungono

secondo *adj.* — second, next

chiesa *f.n.* — church

arte *f.n.* — art

accompagnare — to accompany

lettera *f.n.* — letter

grave *adj.* — heavy, serious

quanto *adv.* — how, how much

conto *m.n.* — account

almeno *conj.* — at least

secolo *m.n.* — century

Unit 17

problema *m.n.*	problem
(*pl.* problemi)	
leggere	to read
io leggo	noi leggiamo
tu leggi	voi leggete
egli legge	loro leggono
piede *m.n.*	foot
specie *f.n.*	species, kind
marito *m.n.*	husband
meglio *adv.*	better
troppo *adj.*	too
studio *m.n.*	study
diritto *m.n.*	right, law
necessario *adj.*	necessary
bastare	to suffice, satisfy
resto *m.n.*	rest, change
attraverso *prep.*	across, through
vi *adv.*	there
avvenire	to happen (conjugated like venire)
governo *m.n.*	government, control
raccogliere	to collect together, gather in
io raccolgo	noi raccogliamo
tu raccogli	voi raccogliete
egli raccoglie	loro raccolgono
spesso *adv.*	often
forma *f.n.*	form
sangue *m.n.*	blood

Unit 18

nessuno *adj.*	no
forte *adj.*	strong
specialmente *adv.*	especially
palazzo *m.n.*	palace
amare	to love
legge *f.n.*	law
infatti *adv.*	in fact
semplice *adj.*	simple
voi *pron.*	you (*pl.*)
viaggio *m.n.*	journey
verità *f.n.*	truth
(*pl.* verità)	
perchè *conj.*	because
dimostrare	to show
tu *pron.*	you (*s.*)
braccio *m.n.s.*	arm
(*pl.* is *f.*: le braccia)	
felice *adj.*	happy
meno *adj.*	less
scuola *f.n.*	school

Unit 19

giovane *adj.*	young
faccia *f.n.*	face
comune *adj.*	common
ripetere	to repeat (conjugated like temere)
signora *f.n.*	Madam, Mrs, lady
importanza *f.n.*	importance
interesse *m.n.*	interest
oro *m.n.*	gold
permettere	to permit (conjugated like mettere)
numero *m.n.*	number
politico *adj.*	political
fermare	to close, stop, fix
incontrare	to meet
vostro *adj.*	your
costituire	to constitute (conjugated like capire)
colore *m.n.*	colour
bisogno *m.n.*	need
quasi *adj.*	almost
notare	to note
ritornare	to return

Unit 20

tuo *adj.*	your
circa *adv.*	about, roughly
notizia *f.n.*	notice, news
moglie *f.n.*	wife
considerare	to consider
veramente *adv.*	really
preparare	to prepare
mentre *m.n.*	moment (in quel mentre, in that moment)
paura *f.n.*	fear
discorso *m.n.*	speech, lecture
libero *adj.*	free
linea *f.n.*	line
profondo *adj.*	deep
tanto *adv.*	so, so much
gruppo *m.n.*	group
fino *adv.*	until, as long as
valere	to be worth
io valgo	noi valiamo
tu vali	voi valete
egli vale	loro valgono
nazionale *adj.*	national
osservare	to observe
durare	to last

Unit 21

sicuro *adj.*	sure, steady.
società *f.n.*	society
(*pl.* società)	
nero *adj.*	black
natura *f.n.*	nature
tutto *adv.*	all, very
giornata *f.n.*	day
te *pron.*	you, to you (*s.*) (te lo promisi, I promised it to you)
genere *m.n.*	kind, genus
breve *adj.*	brief
colpo *m.n.*	blow, kick
quanto *pron.*	how much
posto *m.n.*	position
unico *adj.*	only
fortuna *f.n.*	fortune
domandare	to ask
sala *f.n.*	hall, room
mezzo *m.n.*	half, centre, means
istituto *m.n.*	institute
trarre	to drag, pull
io traggo	noi traiamo
tu trai	voi traete
egli trae	loro traggono

Unit 22

posare	to lay, set down
atto *m.n.*	act
perciò *adv.*	therefore
offrire	to offer
io offro	noi offriamo
tu offri	voi offrite
egli offre	loro offrono
dottore *m.n.*	doctor (medical, academic)
(*f.* dottoressa)	
autore *m.n.*	author
(*f.* autrice)	
misura *f.n.*	measure(ment)
ricevere	to receive (conjugated like temere)
aspetto *m.n.*	appearance, standpoint (sala d'aspetto, waiting room)
età *f.n.*	age, epoch
(*pl.* età)	
fuori *adv.*	outside, except
via *adv.*	away (andare via, to go away)
toccare	to touch, play (an instrument)
tentare	to attempt, tempt
vista *f.n.*	view, sight
muro *m.n.*	wall
(*pl.* muri or *f.* mura)	
mandare	to send
meno *adv.*	less, least, except
necessità *f.n.*	need
(*pl.* necessità)	
potenza *f.n.*	power

Unit 23

controllo *m.n.*	control
aperto *adj.*	open
elemento *m.n.*	element
prima *adv.*	before
caro *adj.*	dear
occupare	to occupy
presente *adj.*	present
ascoltare	to listen
occorrere	to be required (non mi occorre nient' altro, I don't need anything else) (conjugated like correre)
naturale *adj.*	natural
largo *adj.*	wide
fronte *m.n.*	front, brow
formare	to form, instruct
avvertire	to warn, inform (conjugated like sentire)
grosso *adj.*	fat, thick
numeroso *adj.*	numerous
creare	to create
ecco *adv.*	(t)here is, are (ecco! look!)
tavolo *f.n.*	table
simile *adj.*	similar, such
posizione *f.n.*	position
lavorare	to work

Unit 24

grazia *f.n.* — grace, charm (grazie, thanks)

automobile *f.n.* — motor-car (generally replaced colloquially by 'macchina')

porre — to put, place

    io pongo   noi poniamo

    tu poni   voi ponete

    egli pone   loro pongono

moderno *adj.* — modern

rapporto *m.n.* — report, relation

tratto *m.n.* — period, behaviour

ci *adv.* — here, there (non ce ne sono più, there are none left)

    (ce *with* ne)

possibilità *f.n.* — possibility

    (*pl.* possibilità)

onore *m.n.* — honour

volontà *f.n.* — will

    (*pl.* volontà)

proporre — to propose (conjugated like porre)

corso *m.n.* — course, currency

muovere — to move

    io muovo   noi moviamo

    tu muovi   voi movete

    egli muove   loro muovono

basso *adj.* — low

ricordo *m.n.* — memory, souvenir

fede *f.n.* — faith

bianco *adj.* — white, blank

bocca *f.n.* — mouth

davanti *prep.* — in front

consiglio *m.n.* — council, advice

Unit 25

morto *adj.*	dead
attendere	to attend to, wait for (conjugated like prendere)
particolare *adj.*	particular
fratello *m.n.*	brother
ridere	to laugh
io rido	noi ridiamo
tu ridi	voi ridete
egli ride	loro ridono
straordinario *adj.*	extraordinary
scopo *m.n.*	purpose
periodo *m.n.*	period
bambino *m.n.*	little boy (below 8)
metà *f.n.*	half
giovane *f., m.n.*	young person
dieci *num.*	ten
riprendere	to recover, resume (conjugated like prendere)
fine *f.n.*	end
ella *pron.*	she
espressione *f.n.*	expression
passione *f.n.*	passion
fuoco *m.n.*	fire
servizio *m.n.*	service
romano *adj.*	Roman

Unit 26

effetto *m.n.*	effect
dietro *prep.*	behind (dietro richiesta, on request)
aggiungere	to add (conjugated like raggiungere)
superiore *adj.*	superior, higher
cinque *num.*	five
giro *m.n.*	turn, stroll (mettere in giro, to circulate)
mezzo *adj.*	middle, half
giù *adv.*	down(wards)
ottenere	to obtain (conjugated like tenere)
proprio *n.m.*	one's own
scena *f.n.*	scene, stage
udire	to hear
io odo	noi udiamo
tu odi	voi udite
egli ode	loro odono
caldo *adj.*	hot
scendere	to go down, alight (conjugated like prendere)
fermo *adj.*	steady, firm
argomento *m.n.*	argument, subject
molto *adv.*	very, greatly
festa *f.n.*	festival, holiday
accordo *m.n.*	agreement
massimo *adj.*	greatest, supreme
mattina *f.n.*	morning

Unit 27

mantenere	to maintain (conjugated like tenere)
stazione *f.n.*	station
pubblicare	to publish
bene *m.n.*	good
dimenticare	to forget
riferire	to refer (conjugated like capire)
dubbio *m.n.*	doubt
porta *f.n.*	door, gate
funzione *f.n.*	function
davvero *adv.*	really
migliore *adj.*	better (il migliore, the best)
accettare	to accept
assai *adv.*	very much, enough
lingua *f.n.*	tongue, language
fiore *m.n.*	flower
svolgere	to develop, unfold
io svolgo	noi svolgiamo
tu svolgi	voi svolgete
egli svolge	loro svolgono
vasto *adj.*	vast
memoria *f.n.*	memory
desiderio *m.n.*	desire
passo *m.n.*	step, passage

Unit 28

male *m.n.* — evil, illness

sistema *m.n.* — system
    (*pl.* i sistemi)

sentimento *m.n.* — feeling, sensibility

piacere — to please (mi piace, I like it)
    io piaccio   noi piacciamo
    tu piaci   voi piacete
    egli piace   loro piacciono

speciale *adj.* — special

ufficio *m.n.* — office

accadere — to occur,
    accade (3rd pers. sg.) it happens,
    accadde, it happened

due *pron.* — both (tutti e due, both)

chiuso *adj.* — closed

togliere — to take away, remove
    (conjugated like raccogliere)

sviluppo *m.n.* — development

tacere — to be silent (conjugated like piacere)

giardino *m.n.* — garden

riguardare — to concern, look at again

preciso *adj.* — precise

tardi *adv.* — late (*but* il fu Mattia Pascal, the late Mattia Pascal)

cura *f.n.* — care

piazza *f.n.* — square

interessante *adj.* — interesting

giornale *m.n.* — journal, newspaper

Unit 29

oggetto *m.n.*	object
questione *f.n.*	question
poco *adv.*	few, little (fra poco, shortly)
sogno *m.n.*	dream
campagna *f.n.*	country(side), campaign
ritrovare	to recover, find again
assicurare	to assure, insure
relazione *f.n.*	report, relation
certamente *adv.*	certainly
pena *f.n.*	punishment, trouble
dolore *m.n.*	sorrow, pain
vicino *adj.*	near
facile *adj.*	easy
recare	to bring, produce
carta *f.n.*	paper, card, map
santo *adj.*	holy
gioia *f.n.*	happiness, jewel
spiegare	to explain
assai *adj.*	very
giusto *adj.*	just, correct, accurate

Unit 30

difficile *adj.*	difficult
rosso *adj.*	red
divenire	to become (conjugated like venire)
pratico *adj.*	practical
nazione *f.n.*	nation
troppo *adv.*	too much
qua *adv.*	here
scoprire	to discover (conjugated like aprire)
impressione *f.n.*	impression
studiare	to study
importante *adj.*	important
movimento *m.n.*	movement
silenzio *f.n.*	silence
esperienza *f.n.*	experience
lì *adv.*	there
ombra *f.n.*	shade
presto *adv.*	quickly, early
oltre *adv.*	beyond
principe *m.n.*	prince
spingere	to push

io spingo	noi spingiamo
tu spingi	voi spingete
egli spinge	loro spingono

Unit 31

usare	to use
intanto *adv.*	meanwhile
attività *f.n.*	activity
(*pl.* le attività)	
dovere *m.n.*	duty
causa *f.n.*	cause
sorgere	to spring, rise
io sorgo	noi sorgiamo
tu sorgi	voi sorgete
egli sorge	loro sorgono
corrispondere	to correspond (conjugated like rispondere)
sottile *adj.*	thin, subtle
sperare	to hope
lira *f.n.*	lira (currency)
villa *f.n.*	villa, country-house
recente *adj.*	recent
scienza *f.n.*	science
dentro *prep.*	within, inside
concedere	to concede
io concedo	noi concediamo
tu concedi	voi concedete
egli concede	loro concedono
storia *f.n.*	history
naturalmente *adv.*	naturally
nemico *m.n.*	enemy
disporre	to dispose, arrange (conjugated like porre)
fuori *prep.*	outside

Unit 32

realtà *f.n.*	reality
(*pl.* realtà)	
finestra *f.n.*	window
ragazzo *m.n.*	boy
fissare	to fix
prova *f.n.*	proof, examination
decidere	to decide (conjugated like ridere)
povero *adj.*	poor
mangiare	to eat
tuttavia *adv.*	still, nevertheless
presenza *f.n.*	presence
accanto *prep.*	near, beside
intero *adj.*	whole
proposito *m.n.*	intention, resolve (a proposito! by the way!)
puro *adj.*	pure
impedire	to hinder (conjugated like capire)
dinanzi *prep.*	in front
primo *m.n.*	first
sacro *adj.*	holy
mente *f.n.*	mind

Unit 33

macchina *f.n.*	machine, motor-car
pubblico *m.n.*	public
esprimere	to express
io esprimo	noi esprimiamo
tu esprimi	voi esprimete
egli esprime	loro esprimono
albero *m.n.*	tree
peso *m.n.*	weight
concetto *m.n.*	concept
particolare *m.n.*	private, personal (dare particolari, to give details)
eccetera *m.n.*	et cetera
(no plural)	
alzare	to raise, lift
contenere	to contain (conjugated like tenere)
tipo *m.n.*	type, kind
termine *m.n.*	end, boundary
sedere	to sit
io siedo, seggo	noi sediamo
tu siedi	voi sedete
egli siede	loro siedono, seggono
abbandonare	to abandon
triste *adj.*	sad
piuttosto *adv.*	rather
monte *m.n.*	mountain
sopratutto *adv.*	above all
ritorno *m.n.*	return
qualcuno *pron.*	someone, somebody

Unit 34

quanto *adj*.	how much, how many
rivolgere	to turn (over) (conjugated like svolgere)
seguente *adj*.	following
assumere	to undertake, rise, raise
io assumo	noi assumiamo
tu assumi	voi assumete
egli assume	loro assumono
occasione *f.n.*	occasion
salutare	to greet
colui *pron*.	he, he who
letto *m.n.*	bed
dentro *adv*.	within, during (dentro maggio, in May)
difficoltà *f.n.* (*pl*. difficoltà)	difficulty
levare	to raise, remove
lato *m.n.*	side
affare *m.n.*	affair (uomo d'affari, businessman)
spalla *f.n.*	shoulder
nascondere	to hide (conjugated like rispondere)
minuto *m.n.*	minute
leggero *adj*.	light
stella *f.n.*	star
dividere	to divide (conjugated like ridere)
immaginare	to imagine

Unit 35

settimana *f.n.*	week
volto *m.n.*	face
ove *adv.*	where
libertà *f.n.*	liberty
(*pl.* libertà)	
finalmente *adv.*	finally
strano *adj.*	strange
neppure *adv.*	not even
dolce *adj.*	sweet
oh! *interj.*	oh!
dormire	to sleep (conjugated like sentire)
segnare	to mark, note
perfetto *adj.*	perfect
poeta *m.n.*	poet
(*f.n.* poetessa, poetess)	
(*pl.* i poeti)	
fuggire	to flee (conjugated like sentire)
grado *m.n.*	degree, wish (di buon grado, willingly)
possedere	to possess (conjugated like sedere)
musica *f.n.*	music
principio *m.n.*	beginning, principle
mutare	to change
freddo *adj.*	cold

Unit 36

sostenere	to sustain (conjugated like tenere)
conoscenza *f.n.*	acquaintance
succedere	to succeed, happen
io succedo	noi succediamo
tu succedi	voi succedete
egli succede	loro succedono
pregare	to pray, ask
inglese *adj.*	English
sede *f.n.*	seat
inverno *m.n.*	winter
maestro *m.n.*	master, tutor
situazione *f.n.*	situation
ammettere	to admit (conjugated like mettere)
ferro *m.n.*	iron
interessare	to interest
mamma *f.n.*	mother, mama
terzo *adj.*	third
animale *m.n.*	animal
tendere	to stretch (out), spread (conjugated like prendere)
cantare	to sing
motivo *m.n.*	cause, theme
salvare	to save
pronto *adj.*	ready, quick (pronto! hello!)
attenzione *f.n.*	attention

Unit 37

pietà *f.n.*
    (*pl.* pietà)

pity (monte di pietà, pawnbroker's shop)

fiume *m.n.* — river

storico *adj.* — historic

infine *adv.* — finally

cavallo *m.n.* — horse

destino *m.n.* — fate, destination

carne *f.n.* — meat, flesh

significato *m.n.* — meaning

nota *f.n.* — note

liberare — to relieve, liberate

tale *pron.* — such a one

accogliere — to receive, accept (conjugated like raccogliere)

verde *adj.* — green

economico *adj.* — economic

soffrire — to suffer (conjugated like aprire)

maniera *f.n.* — manner, way

italiano *m.n.* — Italian man

avvicinare — to approach

ministro *m.n.* — minister

Unit 38

conservare	to keep, preserve
stretto *adj.*	narrow, strict
sforzo *m.n.*	effort
direttore *m.n.*	director
viso *m.n.*	face
angolo *m.n.*	corner, angle
limitare	to limit
disposizione *f.n.*	disposition
cui *adj.*	whose
evitare	to avoid
fresco *adj.*	fresh, cool
delicato *adj.*	delicate
origine *f.n.*	origin
desiderare	to desire
oscuro *adj.*	dark
costruire	to construct (conjugated like capire)
bere	to drink
io bevo	noi beviamo
tu bevi	voi bevete
egli beve	loro bevono
volume *m.n.*	volume
successo *m.n.*	success, result
zona *f.n.*	zone

Unit 39

lotta *f.n.*	struggle
entro *prep.*	within
alto *m.n.*	height, top
ampio *adj.*	abundant, ample
centro *m.n.*	centre
limite *m.n.*	limit, border
convenire	to suit, be convenient (conviene partire, it is better to leave) (conjugated like venire)
certo *adv.*	certainly
qualcosa *pron.*	something
industria *f.n.*	industry
appartenere	to belong to (conjugated like tenere)
religioso *adj.*	religious
ieri *adv.*	yesterday
iniziare	to begin
pietra *f.n.*	rock
imporre	to impose (conjugated like porre)
patria *f.n.*	native country
serio *adj.*	serious
circolo *m.n.*	circle
ponte *m.n.*	bridge

Unit 40

pagina *f.n.*	page
gioco, giuoco *m.n.*	game, sport, play
cambiare	to (ex)change
immenso *adj.*	immense
vicino *adv.*	close by
discussione *f.n.*	discussion
provare	to try, test, experience, rehearse
uccidere	to kill (conjugated like ridere)
nemmeno *adv.*	not even
senso *m.n.*	sense, direction
temere	to fear (conjugated on Regular Verbs page)
artista *f.*, *m.n.* (*pl.* artisti)	artist
università *f.n.* (*pl.* università)	university
immagine *f.n.*	image
stabilire	to establish (conjugated like capire)
notevole *adj.*	notable
offendere	to offend (conjugated like prendere)

Unit 41

speranza *f.n.*	hope
crescere	to grow
io cresco	noi cresciamo
tu cresci	voi crescete
egli cresce	loro crescono
frase *f.n.*	sentence, phrase
errore *m.n.*	error
pericolo *m.n.*	danger
ridurre	to reduce
io riduco	noi riduciamo
tu riduci	voi riducete
egli riduce	loro riducono
utile *adj.*	useful
uso *m.n.*	use
appunto *adv.*	precisely
niente *m.n.*	nothing
canto *m.n.*	song, side
noto *adj.*	known
scegliere	to choose
io scelgo	noi scegliamo
tu scegli	voi scegliete
egli sceglie	loro scelgono
politica *f.n.*	politics
(*pl.* politica)	
sociale *adj.*	social
principale *adj.*	principal
camminare	to walk, go
pubblico *adj.*	public
domanda *f.n.*	question
indurre	to lead, induce (conjugated like ridurre)

Unit 42

esporre	to expose, exhibit (conjugated like porre)
enorme *adj.*	enormous
terreno *m.n.*	site, ground
difendere	to defend (conjugated like prendere)
passato *m.n.*	past
abito *m.n.*	coat, dress, (monastic) habit
accorgersi	to perceive (mi accorgo che sono sbagliato, I realise I'm wrong) (conjugated like sorgere)
ah! *interj.*	ah!
sguardo *m.n.*	look, glance
risolvere	to resolve
io risolvo	noi risolviamo
tu risolvi	voi risolvete
egli risolve	loro risolvono
ordinare	to order, arrange
estremo *adj.*	extreme
medesimo *adj.*	same
accennare	to indicate
raccontare	to tell
risultato *m.n.*	result
battere	to beat (conjugated like tenere)
grido *m.n.*	shout
esistenza *f.n.*	existence
distruggere	to destroy
io distruggo	noi distruggiamo
tu distruggi	voi distruggete
egli distrugge	loro distruggono

Unit 43

teatro *m.n.*	theatre
legare	to bind
tanto *m.n.*	amount, a certain sum
osservazione *f.n.*	observation
costui *pron.*	that one (*i.e.* man)
stagione *f.n.*	season
classe *f.n.*	class
stanza *f.n.*	room
contare	to count, reckon
manifestare	to reveal, show
civiltà *f.n.*	civilisation
(*pl.* civiltà)	
coprire	to cover (conjugated like aprire)
attorno *prep.*	around
scala *f.n.*	ladder, scale
quadro *m.n.*	picture, square
albergo *m.n.*	hotel
improvviso *adj.*	sudden
ritenere	to retain, hold (back) (conjugated like tenere)
malattia *f.n.*	sickness
procedere	to proceed (conjugated like succedere)

Unit 44

continuo *adj*.	continuous
superare	to overcome (superare gli esami, to pass examinations)
concludere	to conclude (conjugated like chiudere)
inutile *adj*.	useless
preferire	to prefer (conjugated like capire)
collo *m.n.*	neck
produrre	to produce (conjugated like ridurre)
mediterraneo *adj*.	Mediterranean
frutto *m.n.*	fruit, (*fin*.) interest
umanità *f.n.* (*pl*. umanità)	humanity
riportare	to report, return, carry forward
intimo *adj*.	intimate
ramo *m.n.*	branch
soldato *m.n.*	soldier
indicare	to indicate
sereno *adj*.	serene
sollevare	to lift, raise, comfort
vincere	to conquer, defeat, win

io vinco   noi vinciamo
tu vinci   voi vincete
egli vince   loro vincono

Unit 45

compagno *m.n.*	companion
rivelare	to reveal
primavera *f.n.*	spring
conseguenza *f.n.*	consequence
rapido *adj.*	quick
isola *f.n.*	island
virtù *f.n.*	virtue
(*pl.* virtù)	
spettacolo *m.n.*	show, performance
bellezza *f.n.*	beauty
comporre	to compose (conjugated like porre)
folla *f.n.*	crowd
baciare	to kiss
difesa *f.n.*	defence
ognuno *pron.*	everyone
base *f.n.*	base, basis
uguale *adj.*	equal
luna *f.n.*	moon
creatura *f.n.*	creature
commedia *f.n.*	comedy

Unit 46

gusto *m.n.* — taste

piangere — to weep
- io piango
- tu piangi
- egli piange
- noi piangiamo
- voi piangete
- loro piangono

affatto *adv.* — entirely (niente affatto, not at all)

parete *f.n.* — wall

fatica *f.n.* — fatigue, work, trouble

arma *f.n.* — arm, arms
- (*pl.* le armi)

insegnare — to teach

infinito *adj.* — infinite

provvedere — to provide (conjugated like vedere)

aiutare — to help

cattivo *adj.* — bad, naughtly

signorina *f.n.* — Miss, young lady

illustre *adj.* — distinguished, illustrious

gettare — to throw

assoluto *adj.* — absolute

affermare — to assert, affirm

aiuto *m.n.* — help

qualità *f.n.* — quality
- (*pl.* qualità)

riflettere — to reflect
- io rifletto
- tu rifletti
- egli riflette
- noi riflettiamo
- voi riflettete
- loro riflettono

Unit 47

adesso *adv*.	now
minore *adj*.	minor, less, smaller
allontanare	to remove, send away
giudicare	to judge
sorridere	to smile (conjugated like ridere)
padrone *m.n*.	master, owner
ottimo *adj*.	excellent, best
dirigere	to direct, conduct
io dirigo	noi dirigiamo
tu dirigi	voi dirigete
egli dirige	loro dirigono
venti *num*.	twenty
filo *m.n*.	thread, wire
sorella *f.n*.	sister
osare	to dare
proprietà *f.n*.	property
(*pl*. proprietà)	
alcuno *pron*.	somebody, someone, no-one
richiamare	to recall, call back
maggio *m.n*.	May
brutto *m.n*.	ugly, bad, nasty
suono *m.n*.	sound
completamente *adv*.	completely

Unit 48

saluto *m.n.*	greeting
dichiarare	to declare
peccato *m.n.*	sin, shame
attraversare	to cross
riudire	to hear again (conjugated like udire)
epoca *f.n.*	epoch, period
singolare *adj.*	singular
tagliare	to cut
riguardo *m.n.*	regard, consideration
cristiano *adj.*	Christian
cento *num.*	hundred
confermare	to confirm
girare	to turn round, circulate
degno *adj.*	worthy
accendere	to light (accendere la luce, put on the light) (conjugated like prendere)
assistere	to witness, aid (conjugated like esistere)
ricchezza *f.n.*	wealth
tranquillo *adj.*	tranquil
morale *adj.*	moral
animo *m.n.*	mind, courage

Unit 49

produzione *f.n.*	production
appoggiare	to lean, back up
giustizia *f.n.*	justice
importare	to import, be important (non importa, it doesn't matter)
fantasia *f.n.*	fancy, imagination
pagare	to pay
energia *f.n.*	energy
nobile *adj.*	noble
colpa *f.n.*	fault, guilt, blame
traccia *f.n.* (*pl.* tracce)	trace, track
piacere *m.n.*	pleasure
treno *m.n.*	train
scientifico *adj.*	scientific
precedere	to precede (conjugated like temere)
immediato *adj.*	immediate
potente *adj.*	powerful, vigorous
eccellenza *f.n.*	excellence, excellency
metodo *m.n.*	method
intenzione *f.n.*	intention

Unit 50

visitare	to visit
personaggio *m.n.*	personality, character
materiale *m.n.*	material
locale *adj.*	local
avvenimento *m.n.*	occurrence, event
risultare	to result
dente *m.n.*	tooth
tema *m.n.*	subject
(*f.n.* tema, fear)	
milione *num.*	million
dominare	to dominate
considerazione *f.n.*	consideration
biblioteca *f.n.*	library
scrittore *m.n.*	writer
(*f.n.* scrittrice, authoress)	
segretario *m.n.*	(*m.*) secretary
opportuno *adj.*	timely, advisable
comunicare	to communicate
affidare	to entrust
influenza *f.n.*	influence, influenza

Unit 51

lezione *f.n.* — lesson

contadino *m.n.* — countryman

costituzione *f.n.* — constitution

ciascuno *pron.* — everyone

lieve *adj.* — light, soft

direzione *f.n.* — direction

eppure *conj.* — and yet

diffondere — to spread, diffuse

    io diffondo — noi diffondiamo

    tu diffondi — voi diffondete

    egli diffonde — loro diffondono

raro *adj.* — rare

amicizia *f.n.* — friendship

ala *f.n.* — wing

dono *m.n.* — gift

famoso *adj.* — famous

commissione *f.n.* — commission

esatto *adj.* — exact

accorrere — to rush (conjugated like correre)

costruzione *f.n.* — construction

disegno *m.n.* — drawing, design

soluzione *f.n.* — solution

sud *m.n.* — south

Unit 52

giudice *m.n.*	judge
commendatore *m.n.*	Commander
costringere	to force
io costringo	noi costringiamo
tu costringi	voi costringete
egli costringe	loro costringono
finchè *conj.*	until, while
imo *adj.*	deepest, lowest
genio *m.n.*	genius, inclination
(*pl.* geni)	
centrale *adj.*	central
misurare	to measure
Don *m.n.*	honorific for noblemen, priests and criminals
conclusione *f.n.*	conclusion
civile *adj.*	civil
tono *m.n.*	tone
meritare	to merit
giudizio *m.n.*	judgement
reale *adj.*	real, royal
terribile *adj.*	terrible
avvocato *m.n.*	lawyer (barrister, counsel and solicitor)
conquista *f.n.*	conquest
cavaliere *m.n.*	rider, knight
seguito *m.n.*	following, sequel

Unit 53

battaglia *f.n.*	battle
gesto *m.n.*	gesture
fianco *m.n.*	side
visita *f.n.*	visit
avanti *adv.*	before, forward
ricerca *f.n.*	research, enquiry
chilometro *m.n.*	kilometre
volgere	to turn (conjugated like svolgere)
ente *m.n.*	being, board
distinguere	to distinguish
io distinguo	noi distinguiamo
tu distingui	voi distinguete
egli distingue	loro distinguono
stampa *f.n.*	stamp, press, engraving
guardia *f.n.*	guard, protection
fanciullo *m.n.*	boy, child, lad
rilevare	to take away, up, over
montagna *f.n.*	mountain
compagnia *f.n.*	company
estate *f.n.*	summer
commercio *m.n.*	commerce
prezioso *adj.*	precious
aumentare	to increase

Unit 54

progresso *m.n.*	progress
completo *adj.*	complete
pezzo *m.n.*	piece
vittoria *f.n.*	victory
piano *m.n.*	plan, plain, scheme
suonare	to play, sound
caratteristico *adj.*	characteristic
risposta *f.n.*	reply
studioso *m.n.*	scholar
filosofia *f.n.*	philosophy
illuminare	to brighten, lighten
precisamente *adv.*	precisely
onda *f.n.*	wave
sfuggire	to escape, miss (conjugated like sentire)
discendere	to descend (conjugated like prendere)
estero *m.n.*	foreign lands (andare all'estero, to go overseas)
contatto *m.n.*	contact
acquistare	to acquire
coscienza *f.n.*	conscience
filosofo *m.n.*	philosopher

Unit 55

croce *f.n.*	cross
classico *adj.*	classic(al)
impossibile *adj.*	impossible
glorioso *adj.*	glorious
comandare	to order, command
denaro, danaro *m.n.*	money (l'asso di denari, the ace of diamonds)
nave *f.n.*	ship, boat
esame *m.n.*	examination
artistico *adj.*	artistic
nebbia *f.n.*	fog, mist
argento *m.n.*	silver
atmosfera *f.n.*	atmosphere
domani *adv.*	tomorrow
esercito *m.n.*	army
gridare	to shout, shriek
probabilmente *adv.*	probably
agitare	to shake, excite
greco *adj.*	Greek
sezione *f.n.*	section
scorso *adj.*	past (la settimana scorsa, last week)

Unit 56

luminoso *adj.*	shining, luminous
inoltre *adv.*	moreover, besides
vendere	to sell (conjugated like temere)
sostanza *f.n.*	substance, riches
invitare	to invite
contento *adj.*	happy
badare	to take care, pay attention
essere *m.n.*	being, state
meraviglioso *adj.*	marvellous
operare	to operate, act
trascinare	to drag, draw
figliolo, figliuolo *m.n.*	child, son, boy
latte *m.n.*	milk
solito *adj.*	usual
definitivo *adj.*	definitive
abbracciare	to embrace
stringere	to constrain, press (conjugated like costringere)
vuoto *adj.*	empty
qualsiasi *adv.*	whatever, whichever
godere	to enjoy, benefit from
io godo	noi godiamo
tu godi	voi godete
egli gode	loro godono

Unit 57

specchio *m.n.*	mirror
internazionale *adj.*	international
compito *m.n.*	duty, homework
fenomeno *m.n.*	phenomenon
coppia *f.n.*	couple
modesto *adj.*	modest, humble
banco *m.n.*	bench, bank
falso *adj.*	false
discutere	to discuss
io discuto	noi discutiamo
tu discuti	voi discutete
egli discute	loro discutono
male *adj.*	bad, wrong
mistero *m.n.*	mystery
altezza *f.n.*	height (Sua Altezza, Your Highness)
tomba *f.n.*	tomb
finora *adv.*	as yet, hitherto
felicità *f.n.*	happiness
(*pl.* felicità)	
calmo *adj.*	calm
passaggio *m.n.*	passage
generale *m.n.*	general
cammino *m.n.*	way, path, journey
individuo *m.n.*	individual
metro *m.n.*	metre

Unit 58

contemporaneo *adj.*	contemporary
diretto *adj.*	direct
scomparire	to disappear (conjugated like apparire)
teoria *f.n.*	theory
abitare	to inhabit
buttare	to throw
vino *m.n.*	wine
intelligente *adj.*	intelligent
attuale *adj.*	current, real
tedesco *adj.*	German
perfettamente *adv.*	perfectly
rimettere	to replace, defer, remit (conjugated like mettere)
duro *adj.*	hard
determinare	to determine
sicurezza *f.n.*	safety
trattato *m.n.*	treaty
ospite *m.n.*	host, guest
programma *m.n.* (*pl.* programmi)	programme
moto *m.n.*	movement, motion
spegnere	to put out, quench
io spengo	noi spegniamo
tu spegni	voi spegnete
egli spegne	loro spengono

Unit 59

sei *num.*	six
elettrico *adj.*	electric
istante *m.n.*	instant
negare	to deny
nord *m.n.*	north
medico *m.n.*	doctor
potere *m.n.*	power
lieto *adj.*	happy
processo *m.n.*	process, trial
sino *prep.*	until, as far as
parecchio *adj.*	very much, a good many (ne ho parecchio, I have quite a lot)
veste *f.n.*	garment, capacity
educazione *f.n.*	education
derivare	to derive
capace *adj.*	capable, capacious
strappare	to tear away, root out
opporre	to oppose (conjugated like porre)
nuovo *m.n.*	(something) new
popolazione *f.n.*	population
cultura *f.n.*	culture

Unit 60

distanza *f.n.*	distance
cadavere *m.n.*	corpse
otto *num.*	eight
addirittura *adj.*	quite, absolutely
sposare	to marry
capitare	to happen, arrive
orizzonte *m.n.*	horizon
rispetto *m.n.*	respect
giacchè *conj.*	since, now that
regione *f.n.*	region
straniero *adj.*	foreigner
illusione *f.n.*	illusion
pronunciare	to pronounce
grandezza *f.n.*	greatness, size
sano *adj.*	healthy, sane
francese *m.n.*, *f.n.*	Frenchman, Frenchwoman
lanciare	to throw, launch
ingegnere *m.n.*	civil engineer
attaccare	to attack, attach
sette *num.*	seven

Unit 61

doloroso *adj.*	painful, sore
valle *f.n.*	valley
pianura *f.n.*	plain
stanco *adj.*	tired
capello *m.n.*	hair (*s.*) (farsi tagliare i capelli, to have one's hair cut)
ritmo *m.n.*	rhythm
particolarmente *adv.*	particularly
provocare	to provoke
abbastanza *adj.*	sufficient
tradizione *f.n.*	tradition
lontano *adv.*	afar, distantly
legno *m.n.*	wood, log
acuto *adj.*	acute
ve *pron.*	you, to you (used instead of vi before la, le, li, lo and ne)
repubblica *f.n.*	republic
ambiente *m.n.*	surroundings
concezione *f.n.*	conception
scoppiare	to break out, explode
merito *m.n.*	merit
bacio *m.n.*	kiss
raggio *m.n.*	ray

Unit 62

rompere — to break
    io rompo — noi rompiamo
    tu rompi — voi rompete
    egli rompe — loro rompono

rompere	to break
io rompo	noi rompiamo
tu rompi	voi rompete
egli rompe	loro rompono
medio *adj.*	middle, average
spirituale *adj.*	spiritual
fondare	to found
ammirare	to admire
intenso *adj.*	intense
divino *adj.*	divine
serie *f.n.*	series
bile *f.n.*	bile, bad temper
massa *f.n.*	mass
nudo *adj.*	naked
rivedere	to see again, revise (arrivederci!, goodbye!) (conjugated like vedere)
poichè *conj.*	since, because
caffè *m.n.*	coffee
tirare	to pull, draw, shoot at
margine *m.n.*	margin, edge
pane *m.n.*	bread, loaf
assolutamente *adv.*	absolutely
imperatore *m.n.*	emperor
cane *m.n.*	dog
(*f.* cagna, bitch)	
senatore *m.n.*	senator

Unit 63

fondamentale *adj.*	fundamental
amante *m.n.*, *f.n.*	lover
militare *adj.*	military
pranzo *m.n.*	dinner (colloquially, luncheon)
facilmente *adv.*	easily
industriale *adj.*	industrial
arrivo *m.n.*	arrival
riempire, riempiere	to fill (in) (conjugated like capire and temere)
turbare	to trouble
ragazza *f.n.*	girl
eseguire	to execute, perform (conjugated like capire)
sale *m.n.*	salt
petto *m.n.*	chest, breast
pioggia *f.n.*	rain
confessare	to confess
prodotto *m.n.*	product, produce
indagine *f.n.*	enquiry, research
sostituire	to substitute (conjugated like capire)
ipotesi *f.n.*	hypothesis

Unit 64

cima *f.n.*	top, peak
descrivere	to describe (conjugated like scrivere)
unità *f.n.*	unity, unit
(*pl.* unità)	
certezza *f.n.*	certainty
quantità *f.n.*	quantity
(*pl.* quantità)	
eterno *adj.*	eternal
poesia *f.n.*	poem, poetry
costume *m.n.*	costume, custom
grazioso *adj.*	gentle, charming, gracious
documento *m.n.*	document
iniziativa *f.n.*	initiative
circostanza *f.n.*	circumstance
vestire	to dress, put on (mi vesto subito, I'll get dressed now) (conjugated like sentire)
letteratura *f.n.*	literature
istinto *m.n.*	instinct
invito *m.n.*	invitation
dramma *m.n.*	drama
(*pl.* drammi)	
minimo *adj.*	least

Unit 65

oltre *prep*.	beyond, besides
bambina *f.n.*	little girl (below 8)
ringraziare	to thank
mercato *m.n.*	market
avanzare	to advance, put forward
corrente *f.n.*	current, stream
gentile *adj.*	polite, kind
consentire	to agree (conjugated like sentire)
inizio *m.n.*	beginning
ladro *m.n.*	thief
vecchio *m.n.*	old (man)
provincia *f.n.*	province (in provincia, in the country)
duca *m.n.* (*pl.* duchi) (*f.* duchessa)	duke
pratica *f.n.*	experience
umile *adj.*	humble
monumento *m.n.*	monument
precedente *adj.*	preceding
nervoso *adj.*	nervous
mattino *m.n.*	morning

Unit 66

morto *m.n.*	dead person
regno *m.n.*	kingdom, reign
lago *m.n.*	lake
agire	to act (conjugated like capire)
prossimo *adj.*	next
lento *adj.*	slow
carità *f.n.*	charity
(*pl.* carità)	
giovinezza *f.n.*	youth
colpire	to strike (conjugated like capire)
operazione *f.n.*	operation
nominare	to nominate, name
percorrere	to travel, cover (conjugated like correre)
cervello *m.n.*	brain
attesa *f.n.*	expectation (sala d'attesa, waiting room)
ferire	to wound (conjugated like capire)
rientrare	to return home, re-enter
rete *f.n.*	net(work)
arrestare	to arrest, stop
male *adv.*	badly

Unit 67

penetrare	to penetrate
resistenza *f.n.*	resistance
differenza *f.n.*	difference
relativo *adj.*	relative
contrasto *m.n.*	contrast
elevare	to raise
affetto *m.n.*	affection
rivoluzione *f.n.*	revolution
cessare	to cease
tesoro *m.n.*	treasure, treasury
opinione *f.n.*	opinion
proseguire	to continue, pursue (conjugated like seguire)
strumento *m.n.*	instrument
dedicare	to dedicate
perdita *f.n.*	loss
rilievo *m.n.*	relief
vittima *f.n.*	victim
parente *m.n.*	relative
sospetto *m.n.*	suspect person, suspicion
conte *m.n.*	count
(*f.* contessa)	

Unit 68

autorità *f.n.*	authority
(*pl.* autorità)	
suolo *m.n.*	soil, ground
pomeriggio *m.n.*	afternoon
guidare	to guide
evidente *adj.*	evident
cappello *m.n.*	hat
sorriso *m.n.*	smile
mezzogiorno *m.n.*	midday, south
neanche *adv.*	not even
comunicazione *f.n.*	communication
prestare	to lend, render
titolo *m.n.*	title
febbre *f.n.*	fever
preghiera *f.n.*	prayer
giugno *m.n.*	June
data *f.n.*	date
eroe *m.n.*	hero
subire	to suffer, undergo (conjugated like sentire)
violento *adj.*	violent

Unit 69

conversazione *f.n.*	conversation
mille *num.*	thousand
europeo *adj.*	European
imparare	to learn
lungo *adv.*	slowly, tediously
detto *adj.*	said
fisso *adj.*	fixed
precipitare	to hasten, hurl down
spazio *m.n.*	space
biglietto *m.n.*	ticket
secco *adj.*	dry
direttamente *adv.*	directly
innanzi *prep.*	before
solere	to be accustomed
io soglio	noi sogliamo
tu suoli	voi solete
egli suole	loro sogliono
bosco *m.n.*	wood
significare	to mean
lungo *prep.*	along
comperare	to buy
bruno *adj.*	brown
fiducia *f.n.*	confidence, trust

Unit 70

mestiere *m.n.*	trade, occupation
esercitare	to exercise
ragionare	to discuss, chat
armonia *f.n.*	harmony
fiamma *f.n.*	flame
convincere	to convince (conjugated like vincere)
castello *m.n.*	castle
insomma *adv.*	briefly, in short
spesa *f.n.*	expense, shopping
dapprima *adv.*	at first
volare	to fly
oriente *m.n.*	east, Orient
alba *f.n.*	dawn
cittadino *m.n.*	citizen
suo *pron.*	his own, her own (dalla sua, on his side)
pericoloso *adj.*	dangerous
curiosità *f.n.* (*pl.* curiosità)	curiosity
cupo *adj.*	dark, deep, hollow
trattenere	to hold back, detain (conjugated like tenere)
manifestazione *f.n.*	manifestation, exhibition

Unit 71

raccomandare	to recommend, entrust (posta raccomandata, registered post)
povero *m.n.*	pauper, poor man
grano *m.n.*	grain, corn
gloria *f.n.*	glory
confronto *m.n.*	comparison
regola *f.n.*	rule, regulation
lassù *adv.*	up there
stasera *adv.*	tonight
fatto *adj.*	made, grown (a cose fatte, too late)
crisi *f.n.*	crisis
allegro *adj.*	lively, merry
bruciare	to burn
rosa *f.n.*	rose
indipendenza *f.n.*	independence
ospedale *m.n.*	hospital
edificio *m.n.*	building
ruota, rota *f.n.*	wheel
scambio *m.n.*	exchange
cogliere	to pick, pluck, take (conjugated like raccogliere)

Unit 72

svegliare	to arouse, wake up
esaminare	to examine
tuttora *adv.*	still, again
responsabile *adj.*	responsible
favore *m.n.*	favour
solenne *adj.*	solemn
colonna *f.n.*	column
impresa *f.n.*	enterprise, firm
invocare	to invoke
splendore *m.n.*	brightness
odore *m.n.*	smell
collocare	to place, dispose of
buio *m.n.*	darkness
accostare	to accost, approach
ufficiale *m.n.*	official, officer
altrettanto *adv.*	as many, as much (altrettanto! the same to you!)
pallido *adj.*	pale
cenno *n.m.*	sign, mention
applicazione *f.n.*	application
sciogliere	to dissolve, loosen (conjugated like raccogliere)

Unit 73

porto *m.n.*	port
ingresso *m.n.*	entrance
organizzazione *f.n.*	organisation
destra *f.n.*	right-hand side
tragico *adj.*	tragic
supporre	to suppose (conjugated like porre)
categoria *f.n.*	category
pianta *f.n.*	plan, map, plant
complicato *adj.*	complicated
scarso *adj.*	scarce, insufficient
calma *f.n.*	calmness
attacco *m.n.*	attack
marmo *m.n.*	marble
provenire	to derive, proceed (conjugated like venire)
evidentemente *adv.*	evidently
procurare	to obtain, attempt
fornire	to furnish, provide with (conjugated like capire)
orientale *adj.*	eastern, oriental
respiro *m.n.*	breath, respite
tremare	to tremble

Unit 74

immobile *adj.*	motionless (beni immobili, real estate)
consistere	to consist of (conjugated like esistere)
scambiare	to exchange
cimitero *m.n.*	cemetery
adoperare	to use
progetto *m.n.*	project
pubblicazione *f.n.*	publication
congiungere	to join, connect (conjugated like raggiungere)
rapidamente *adv.*	rapidly
chiarire	to clarify, explain (conjugated like capire)
prevedere	to foresee, expect (conjugated like vedere)
giocare	to play
consigliare	to advise
umido *adj.*	wet, humid
attimo *m.n.*	moment
proprietario *m.n.*	proprietor
avvenire	to happen, occur (conjugated like venire)
orologio *m.n.*	clock
cortile *m.n.*	courtyard
domenica *f.n.*	Sunday

Unit 75

abitudine *f.n.*	habit
domino *m.n.*	domino (mask), dominoes
giovare	to benefit, be of use
collegio *m.n.*	college
miracolo *m.n.*	miracle
indipendente *adj.*	independent
contribuire	to contribute (conjugated like capire)
dio *m.n.* (*pl.* gli dei)	god, God
confine *m.n.*	frontier, limit
naso *m.n.*	nose
coraggio *m.n.*	courage
escludere	to exclude (conjugated like chiudere)
partito *m.n.*	party, side
gatto *m.n.*	cat
riposo *m.n.*	rest
consegnare	to deliver
colonnello *m.n.*	colonel
prato *m.n.*	meadow
viaggiatore *m.n.*	traveller

Unit 76

sviluppare	to develop
vestito *m.n.*	dress, suit
citare	to cite
modello *m.n.*	model
dicembre *m.n.*	December
onde *adv.*	whence, by which
unito *adj.*	united
lettore *m.n.*	reader
(*f.* lettrice)	
membro *m.n.*	member
(*f.pl.* in anatomy, le membra)	
labbro *m.n.*	lip
(*f.pl.* le labbra)	
costo *m.n.*	cost
vuoto *m.n.*	void
tè *m.n.*	tea
costa *f.n.*	coast
agosto *m.n.*	August
fedele *adj.*	faithful
interno *adj.*	inner, interior
fase *f.n.*	phase

Unit 77

piegare	to fold
sensibilità *f.n.*	sensibility
(*pl.* sensibilità)	
lusso *m.n.*	luxury, extravagance
presidente *m.n.*	president
velo *m.n.*	veil
intelligenza *f.n.*	intelligence
stamane *adv.*	this morning
partenza *f.n.*	departure
impero *m.n.*	empire
coloniale *adj.*	colonial
destinare	to destine, address (a letter)
vicenda *f.n.*	event, turn
trenta *num.*	thirty
volo *m.n.*	flight
arco *m.n.*	arch, bow
lentamente *adv.*	slowly
cattolico *adv.*	Catholic
zio *m.n.*	uncle
insegnamento *m.n.*	teaching

Unit 78

richiedere	to send for, require (conjugated like chiedere)
corsa *f.n.*	race, run
ritratto *m.n.*	portrait
seguitare	to continue, follow up
trincea *f.n.*	trench
sorprendere	to surprise (conjugated like prendere)
straniero *m.n.*	foreigner
trasformare	to transform
sorte *f.n.*	luck, fortune
organo *m.n.*	organ
tristezza *f.n.*	sadness
tenero *adj.*	tender
cacciare	to hunt, banish, drive away
promettere	to promise (conjugated like mettere)
cameriera *f.n.*	waitress, chambermaid
orgoglio *m.n.*	pride
sempre *adj.*	ever-
commettere	to commit (conjugated like mettere)
vago *adj.*	indistinct, erratic, charming
paterno *adj.*	paternal
velocità *f.n.* (*pl.* velocità)	speed

Unit 79

esterno *adj.*	outer, exterior
promessa *f.n.*	promise
indirizzo *m.n.*	address
freddo *adj.*	cold
separare	to separate
celebre *adj.*	celebrated
atteggiamento *m.n.*	attitude, behaviour
rigido *adj.*	rigid
articolo *m.n.*	article
primitivo *adj.*	primitive
elegante *adj.*	elegant
catena *f.n.*	chain
cinematografo *m.n.*	cinema, pictures
tentativo *m.n.*	attempt
lavoratore *m.n.*	worker
(*f.* lavoratrice)	
rumore *m.n.*	noise
maschera *f.n.*	mask
ingannare	to deceive
specie *adv.*	especially
radio *f.n.*	radio, broadcasting

Unit 80

banca *f.n.*	bank
economia *f.n.*	economy, economics
rinnovare	to renew
carica *f.n.*	charge, employment
ingegno *m.n.*	genius, talent
centinaio *m.n.*	hundred
(*f.pl.* centinaia)	
pastore *m.n.*	shepherd, minister
determinato *adj.*	stated, definite
romanzo *m.n.*	novel
collega *m.n.*, *f.n.*	colleague
(*pl.* colleghi)	
fascio *m.n.*	bunch, bundle, sheaf
meraviglia *f.n.*	marvel
accusare	to accuse, acknowledge
corda *f.n.*	rope, string
miseria *f.n.*	misery, penury
immediatamente *adv.*	immediately
resistere	to resist (conjugated like esistere)
originale *adj.*	original
latino *adj.*	Latin

Unit 81

blocco *m.n.*	block
richiamo *m.n.*	recall, summons
seno *m.n.*	bosom
partecipare	to participate
servo *m.n.*	servant
dignità *f.n.*	dignity, self-respect
(*pl.* dignità)	
staccare	to detach, pull off
rivista *f.n.*	review, magazine
misterioso *adj.*	mysterious
novembre *m.n.*	November
privato *adj.*	private
riva *f.n.*	bank, shore
stesso *pron.*	oneself, himself, herself
simbolo *m.n.*	symbol
fila *f.n.*	row
superficie *f.n.*	surface
(*pl.* superfici, superficie)	
punta *f.n.*	point, tip
messa *f.n.*	placing, Mass
constatare	to ascertain, authenticate

Unit 82

contributo *m.n.*	contribution
affrontare	to confont, face
barba *f.n.*	beard
prezzo *m.n.*	price
qualunque *adj.*	whatever
carro *m.n.*	cart, van
definire	to define, resolve (conjugated like finire)
condannare	to condemn
fattore *m.n.*	agent, maker
continente *m.n.*	continent
sacrificio *m.n.*	sacrifice
incominciare	to begin
ottobre *m.n.*	October
grigio *adj.*	grey
vestito *adj.*	dressed
lucido *adj.*	bright, brilliant
odio *m.n.*	hatred
critico *adj.*	critical
aprile *m.n.*	April
assegnare	to assign, grant

Unit 83

moda *f.n.*	fashion
respingere	to repel, repulse
io respingo	noi respingiamo
tu respingi	voi respingete
egli respinge	loro respingono
comitato *m.n.*	committee
fango *m.n.*	mud
commerciale *adj.*	commercial
fabbrica *f.n.*	factory
singolo *adj.*	single
ispirare	to inspire
santo *m.n.*	saint
introdurre	to introduce (conjugated like ridurre)
disciplina *f.n.*	discipline
informare	to inform
nido *m.n.*	nest
oppure *adv.*	or
stupore *m.n.*	amazement
onorevole *m.n.*	parliamentary deputy
dato *m.n.*	fact
disgrazia *f.n.*	disgrace, accident
ammirazione *f.n.*	admiration
suggerire	to suggest (conjugated like capire)

Unit 84

frequente *adj.*	frequent
richiesta *f.n.*	request, demand
contenuto *m.n.*	contents
commozione *f.n.*	emotion, commotion
trascurare	to disregard, overlook
raccolta *f.n.*	collection, harvest
voltare	to turn, change round
grandioso *adj.*	majestic, stately
abbassare	to lower, reduce
soglia *f.n.*	threshold
chiave *f.n.*	key
regolare	to regulate
sensazione *f.n.*	sensation
seta *f.n.*	silk
aumento *m.n.*	increase
severo *adj.*	severe
vergogna *f.n.*	shame
congresso *m.n.*	congress
sedia *f.n.*	chair, seat
abbandono *m.n.*	abandonment, waiving
comparire	to appear, attend (conjugated like apparire)

Unit 85

curioso *adj.*	curious
dottrina *f.n.*	doctrine
fama *f.n.*	fame, reputation
americano *adj.*	American
esaltare	to exalt, extol
formazione *f.n.*	formation, creation
salute *f.n.*	health, welfare
inferiore *adj.*	lower, inferior
maschio *m.n.*	male
informazione *f.n.*	information
scorgere	to perceive (conjugated like sorgere)
affacciare	to indicate
voglia *f.n.*	wish, desire
statua *f.n.*	statue
nonchè *adv.*	even less
dimostrazione *f.n.*	demonstration
comodo *adj.*	comfortable
ministero *m.n.*	ministry
deporre	to deposit, depose (conjugated like porre)
retta *f.n.*	attention, straight line

Unit 86

estendere	to extend (conjugated like prendere)
polvere *f.n.*	dust, powder
scorrere	to glide, glance at, elapse (conjugated like correre)
netto *adj.*	clean, clear (prezzo netto, net price)
fonte *f.n.*	source, fountain
basilica *f.n.*	basilica
futuro *adj.*	future
peggio *adv.*	worse
spiegazione *f.n.*	explanation
tronco *m.n.*	trunk
conferenza *f.n.*	lecture, conference
cerchio *m.n.*	circle
stilo *m.n.*	style
rammentare	to recall, remind
entrambi *pron.*	both
indispensabile *adj.*	indispensable
volentieri *adv.*	willingly
odiare	to hate
osservatore *m.n.* (*f.* osservatrice)	observer

Unit 87

scarpa *f.n.*	shoe, scarp
capitolo *m.n.*	chapter
settembre *m.n.*	September
bravo *adj.*	able, plucky, clever
altrimenti *adv.*	otherwise
personale *adj.*	personal
avvolgere	to roll up, wind (conjugated like svolgere)
scritto *m.n.*	writing
risalire	to rise (again), trace back (conjugated like salire)
simpatico *adj.*	nice, congenial
divertire	to amuse, entertain (conjugated like sentire)
spargere	to spread, scatter
io spargo	noi spargiamo
tu spargi	voi spargete
egli sparge	loro spargono
novità	novelty
(*pl.* novità)	
capitale *m.n.*	capital (financial)
(*f.* capitale, capital (city))	
miglio *m.n.*	mile, millet
danno *m.n.*	damage, injury
ripartire	to leave, distribute (conjugated like partire)
complesso *adj.*	complex

Unit 88

metallico *adj.*	metallic
fiero *adj.*	proud, severe, fierce
prigione *f.n.*	prison
facoltà *f.n.*	faculty
(*pl.* facoltà)	
gamba *f.n.*	leg
distinto *adj.*	distinguished, refined
soffocare	to suffocate
fisico *adj.*	physical
amministrazione *f.n.*	administration
rovesciare	to overthrow, overturn
talvolta *adv.*	sometimes
provvedimento *m.n.*	precaution
tecnica *f.n.*	technique
unione *f.n.*	union
racconto *m.n.*	story
camicia *f.n.*	shirt
formula *f.n.*	formula
visione *f.n.*	vision
guaio *m.n.*	woe, fix

Unit 89

fotografia *f.n.*	photograph(y)
quando *m.n.*	time
malato *adj.*	ill
complesso *m.n.*	complex
paradiso *m.n.*	paradise
meravigliare	to marvel
timore *m.n.*	fear, dread
vizio *m.n.*	vice
quarto *m.n.*	quarter
sonno *m.n.*	sleep
dito *m.n.*	finger
(*pl.* usu. *f.* le dita)	
persuadere	to persuade
io persuado	noi persuadiamo
tu persuadi	voi persuadete
egli persuade	loro persuadono
bestia *f.n.*	beast
consumare	to wear out, consume
ivi *adv.*	there
preparazione *f.n.*	preparation
invece *prep.*	instead
finito *adj.*	finished
femmina *f.n.*	female, woman

Unit 90

fuga *f.n.*	flight, escape
laggiù *adv.*	down there
norma *f.n.*	rule, norm, guidance
missione *f.n.*	mission
coro *m.n.*	chorus
legato *adj.*	bound, tied
collina *f.n.*	hill
azzurro *adj.*	blue
sparire	to disappear (conjugated like apparire)
scandalo *m.n.*	scandal
trascorrere	to pass (time), spend, go through (conjugated like correre)
febbraio *m.n.*	February
sasso *m.n.*	stone
gioventù *f.n.* (*pl.* gioventù)	young people, youth
frutta *f.n.* (*pl.* frutta, frutte)	fruit
rifare	to do again, rebuild, make good
fumo *m.n.*	smoke

Unit 91

magari *adv.*
maybe, would it were thus!

ballo *m.n.*
ball, dance

eccezionale *adj.*
exceptional

ansia *f.n.*
anxiety

piovere
to rain (only 3rd person sg. of each tense; conjugated like bere)

maturo *adj.*
ripe

cedere
to yield
- io cedo
- tu cedi
- egli cede
- noi cediamo
- voi cedete
- loro cedono

essenzialmente *adv.*
essentially

diminuire
to diminish, reduce (conjugated like capire)

papa *m.n.*
(*pl.* i papi)
pope

improvvisamente *adv.*
suddenly

dipendere
to depend (conjugated like prendere)

ironia *f.n.*
irony

accanto *adv.*
close by, nearby

lampada *f.n.*
lamp

semplicemente *adv.*
simply

universitario *adj.*
university

solido *adj.*
solid

cinquanta *num.*
fifty

Unit 92

calore *m.n.*	heat
distribuire	to distribute (conjugated like capire)
sincero *adj.*	sincere
affrettare	to quicken
eguale *adj.*	equal
domestico *adj.*	domestic
silenzioso *adj.*	silent
materiale *adj.*	material
siccome *conj.*	since, as
telegramma *m.n.* (*pl.* telegrammi)	telegram
vetro *m.n.*	glass
patto *m.n.*	pact
terminare ·	to finish, terminate
adottare	to adopt
protagonista *m.n.* (*pl.* protagonisti)	protagonist
impiegare	to employ
privo *adj.*	lacking, devoid

Unit 93

normale *adj.*	normal
logica *f.n.*	logic
essenziale *adj.*	essential
marchese *m.n.*	marquis
(*f.* marchesa)	
verso *m.n.*	(line of) verse
migliaio *m.n.*	thousand
(*pl.* migliaia)	
sinistra *adj.*	left
omaggio *m.n.*	homage
colei *pron.*	she who
forno *m.n.*	oven, furnace
caccia *f.n.*	hunt(ing)
villaggio *m.n.*	village
perdonare	to forgive
genitore *n.m.*	parent
(*f.* genitrice)	
conquistare	to conquer
mortale *adj.*	mortal
criterio *m.n.*	criterion
scuro *adj.*	dark

Unit 94

indicazione *f.n.*	indication
combattere	to fight (conjugated like temere)
innocente *adj.*	innocent
umore *m.n.*	humour
nuvola *f.n.*	cloud
(*also* nuvolo *m.n.*)	
fame *f.n.*	hunger
acceso *adj.*	lit
cerimonia *f.n.*	ceremony
recentemente *adv.*	recently
doppio *adj.*	double
cassa *f.n.*	box, case, cashier's desk
terzo *m.n.*	third, third party
rubare	to steal
compagna *f.n.*	female companion
sostare	to pause, stop
continuamente *adv.*	continually, continuously
ultimo *pron.*	last
corte *f.n.*	court(yard)
eleganza *f.n.*	elegance

Unit 95

violenza *f.n.*	violence
costante *adj.*	constant
religione *f.n.*	religion
fretta *f.n.*	haste
tesi *f.n.*	thesis
(*pl.* tesi)	
saltare	to leap
diavolo *m.n.*	devil
abbastanza *adv.*	sufficiently
lembo *m.n.*	edge, border
dimensione *f.n.*	dimension
sentimentale *adj.*	sentimental
arabo *adj.*	Arab, Arabic
furia *f.n.*	fury
circondare	to surround
leggenda *f.n.*	legend
vaso *m.n.*	pot, vase
campana *f.n.*	bell
cancello *m.n.*	railing, gate
aspro *adj.*	harsh, tart

Unit 96

tracciare	to trace
subito *adj.*	sudden
occidentale *adj.*	western
segreto *m.n.*	secret
inviare	to send
coperto *adj.*	covered
ulteriore *adj.*	further, ulterior
commuovere, commovere	to affect, excite (conjugated like muovere)
regolare *adj.*	regular
realmente *adv.*	really, royally
marittimo *adj.*	maritime
neve *f.n.*	snow
esercizio *m.n.*	exercise
sfruttare	to exploit, exhaust
dettare	to dictate
ricominciare	to start again
uccello *m.n.*	bird
provvisorio *adj.*	provisional, temporary
o! *interj.*	o!
suscitare	to provoke, rouse

Unit 97

taluno *adj.*	some
altresì *adv.*	also, likewise
fascista *adj.*	fascist
solco *m.n.*	furrow, wake (of ship)
tecnico *adj.*	technical
tetto *m.n.*	roof
reggere	to rule, support, endure (conjugated like leggere)
capitano *m.n.*	captain
tradurre	to translate (conjugated like ridurre)
debito *m.n.*	debt
difetto *m.n.*	defect
opposto *adj.*	opposite, contrary
esperimento *m.n.*	experiment, trial
devoto *adj.*	pious, devout
perduto *adj.*	lost
individuale *adj.*	individual
incoraggiare	to encourage
generazione *f.n.*	generation
intorno *adv.*	around
debole *adj.*	weak

Unit 98

regina *f.n.*	queen
maestà *f.n.*	majesty
(*pl.* maestà)	
lavare	to wash
diffuso *adj.*	diffuse, broadcast
critica *f.n.*	criticism
positivo *adj.*	positive
prigioniero *m.n.*	prisoner
premere	to press, urge (conjugated like temere)
sepolcro *m.n.*	tomb, vault
vicinanza *f.n.*	neighbourhood
solito *m.n.*	usual (fuori del solito, out of the ordinary)
reciproco *adj.*	reciprocal
amoroso *adj.*	amorous
personalità *f.n.*	personality
(*pl.* personalità)	
eco *f.* or *m.n.*	echo
(*pl.* gli echi)	
canale *m.n.*	canal, Channel (*but* la Manica, English Channel)
ginocchio *m.n.*	knee
(*pl.* le ginocchia)	

Unit 99

ardente *adj.*	burning
sacco *m.n.*	sack, bag
celeste *adj.*	heavenly, sky-blue
sparare	to shoot, fire
destare	to awake, stir
senato *m.n.*	senate
apparecchio *m.n.*	apparatus, aeroplane
sinistro *adj.*	left, ominous
gennaio *m.n.*	January
carico *m.n.*	load, charge
incontro *prep.*	towards
sposa *f.n.*	bride
promuovere	to promote (conjugated like commuovere)
giovanile *adj.*	juvenile
simpatia *f.n.*	sympathy, liking
roccia *f.n.*	rock
(*pl.* rocce)	
apparenza *f.n.*	appearance
avventura *f.n.*	adventure
illustrare	to illustrate
bianco *m.n.*	whiteness, white man

Unit 100

sorpresa *f.n.*	surprise
paesaggio *m.n.*	landscape
mancanza *f.n.*	lack, absence
incerto *adj.*	uncertain
prima *f.n.*	first (class), première
eccezione *f.n.*	exception
matrimonio *m.n.*	marriage, wedding
reparto *m.n.*	department, (military) detachment
robusto *adj.*	robust
ignoto *adj.*	unknown
assorbire	to absorb (conjugated like capire)
gola *f.n.*	throat
tenerezza *f.n.*	tenderness
logico *adj.*	logical
tensione *f.n.*	tension
onorevole *adj.*	honourable
vano *adj.*	vain
collaborazione *f.n.*	collaboration
calmare	to calm
disegnare	to draw, design

Italian Index

attraversare 48
attraverso 17
attuale 58
aumentare 53
aumento 84
automobile 24
autore 22
autorità 68
avanti 53
avanzare 65
avere 1
avvenimento 50
avvenire 17, 74
avventura 99
avvertire 23
avvicinare 37
avvocato 52
avvolgere 87
azione 15
azzurro 90

baciare 45
bacio 61
badare 56
ballo 91
bambina 65
bambino 25
banca 80
banco 57
barba 82
base 45
basilica 86
basso 24
bastare 17
battaglia 53
battere 42
bellezza 45
bello 6
bene 7, 27
bere 38
bestia 89
bianco 24, 99
biblioteca 50
biglietto 69
bile 62

bisognare 11
bisogno 19
blocco 81
bocca 24
bosco 69
braccia 18
braccio 18
bravo 87
breve 21
bruciare 71
bruno 69
brutto 47
buio 72
buono 7
buttare 58

caccia 93
cacciare 78
cadavere 60
cadere 15
caffè 62
caldo 26
calma 73
calmare 100
calore 92
cambiare 40
camera 13
cameriera 78
camicia 88
camminare 41
campagna 29
campana 95
campo 14
canale 98
cancello 95
cane 62
cantare 36
canto 41
capace 59
capello 61
capire 16
capitale 87
capitano 97
capitare 60
capitolo 87

cappello 68
carattere 15
caratteristico 54
carica 80
carico 99
carità 66
came 37
caro 23
carro 82
carta 29
casa 6
caso 10
cassa 94
castello 70
categoria 73
catena 79
cattivo 46
cattolico 77
causa 31
cavaliere 52
cavallo 37
cedere 91
celebre 79
celeste 99
cenno 72
centinaia 80
centinaio 80
cento 48
centrale 52
centro 39
cercare 9
cerchio 86
cerimonia 94
certamente 29
certezza 64
certo 7, 39
cervello 66
cessare 67
che 1
chi 7
chiamare 8
chiarire 74
chiaro 14
chiave 84
chiedere 12
chiesa 16
chilometro 53

chiudere 14
chiuso 28
ci 3, 24
ciascuno 51
cielo 14
cima 64
cimitero 74
cinematografo 79
cinquanta 91
cinque 26
ciò 8
cioè 12
circa 20
circolo 39
circondare 95
circostanza 64
citare 76
città 8
cittadino 70
civile 52
civiltà 43
classe 43
classico 55
cogliere 71
colei 93
collaborazione 100
collega 80
collegio 75
collina 90
collo 44
collocare 72
coloniale 77
colonna 72
colonnello 75
colore 19
colpa 49
colpire 66
colpo 21
colui 34
comandare 55
combattere 94
come 2, 4
cominciare 10
comitato 83
commedia 45
commendatore 52
commerciale 83

commercio 53
commettere 78
commissione 51
commovere 96
commozione 84
commuovere 96
comodo 85
compagna 94
compagnia 53
compagno 45
comparire 84
comperare 69
compiere 15
compito 57
complesso 87, 89
completamente 47
completo 54
complicato 73
comporre 45
comprendere 13
comune 19
comunicare 50
comunicazione 68
con 1
concedere 31
concetto 33
concezione 61
concludere 44
conclusione 52
condannare 82
condizione 15
condurre 14
conferenza 86
confermare 48
confessare 63
confine 75
confronto 71
congiungere 74
congresso 84
conoscenza 36
conoscere 10
conquista 52
conquistare 93
consegnare 75
conseguenza 45
consentire 65
conservare 38

considerare 20
considerazione 50
consigliare 74
consiglio 24
consistere 74
constatare 81
consumare 89
contadino 51
contare 43
contatto 54
conte 67
contemporaneo 58
contenere 33
contento 56
contenuto 84
contessa 67
continente 82
continuamente 94
continuo 44
contrasto 67
contribuire 75
contributo 82
contro 8
controllo 23
conversazione 69
convincere 70
coperto 96
coppia 57
coprire 43
coraggio 75
corda 80
coro 90
corpo 13
corrente 65
correre 13
corrispondere 31
corsa 78
corso 24
corte 94
cortile 74
coscienza 54
così 4
costa 76
costante 95
costituire 19
costituzione 51
costo 76

costringere 54
costruire 38
costruzione 51
costui 43
costume 64
creare 23
creatura 45
credere 8
crescere 41
crisi 71
cristiano 48
criterio 93
critica 98
critico 82
croce 55
cui 4, 38
cultura 59
cuore 10
cupo 70
cura 28
curiosità 70
curioso 85

da 1
danaro 55
danno 87
dapprima 70
data 68
dato 83
davanti 24
davvero 27
debito 97
debole 97
dedicare 67
definire 82
definitivo 56
degno 48
dei 75
delicato 38
denaro 55
dente 50
dentro 31, 34
deporre 85
derivare 59
descrivere 64

desiderare 38
desiderio 27
destare 99
destino 37
destra 73
determinare 58
determinato 80
dettare 96
detto 69
devoto 97
di 1
diavolo 95
dicembre 76
dichiarare 48
dieci 25
dietro 26
difendere 42
difesa 45
difetto 97
difficile 30
difficoltà 34
diffondere 51
diffuso 98
dignità 81
dimensione 95
dimenticare 27
diminuire 91
dimostrare 18
dimostrazione 86
dinanzi 32
dio 75
dipendere 91
dire 2
direttamente 69
diretto 58
direzione 51
dirigere 47
diritto 17
discendere 54
disciplina 83
discorso 20
discussione 40
discutere 57
disegnare 100
disegno 51
disgrazia 83
disporre 31

disposizione 38
distanza 60
distinguere 53
distinto 88
distribuire 92
distruggere 42
dita 89
dito 89
divenire 30
diventare 11
diverso 12
divertire 87
dividere 34
divino 62
documento 64
dolce 35
dolore 29
doloroso 61
domanda 41
domandare 21
domani 57
domenica 74
domestico 92
dominare 50
domino 75
Don 52
donna 8
dono 51
dopo 5
doppio 94
dormire 35
dottore 22
dottrina 85
dove 5
dovere 2, 31
dramma 64
dubbio 27
duca 65
due 3, 28
dunque 13
durante 13
durare 20
duro 58

e 1
eccellenza 49
eccetera 33
eccezionale 91
eccezione 100
ecco 23
eco 98
economia 80
economico 37
edificio 71
educazione 59
effetto 26
egli 5
eguale 92
elegante 79
eleganza 94
elemento 23
elettrico 59
elevare 67
ella 25
energia 49
enorme 42
ente 53
entrambi 86
entrare 10
entro 39
epoca 48
eppure 51
eroe 68
errore 41
esaltare 85
esame 55
esaminare 72
esatto 51
escludere 75
eseguire 63
esempio 16
esercitare 70
esercito 55
esercizio 96
esistenza 42
esistere 13
esperienza 30
esperimento 97
esporre 42
espressione 25
esprimere 33

essa 6
essenziale 93
essenzialmente 91
essere 1, 56
esso 6
estate 53
estendere 86
esterno 79
estremo 42
età 22
eterno 64
europeo 69
evidente 68
evidentemente 73
evitare 38

fabbrica 83
faccia 19
facile 29
facilmente 63
facoltà 88
falso 57
fama 85
fame 94
famiglia 12
famoso 51
fanciullo 53
fango 83
fantasia 49
fare 2
fascio 80
fascista 97
fase 76
fatica 46
fatto 9, 71
fattore 82
favore 72
febbraio 90
febbre 68
fede 24
fedele 76
felice 18
felicità 57
femmina 89
fenomeno 57

ferire 36
fermare 19
fermo 26
ferro 36
festa 26
fiamma 70
fianco 53
fiducia 69
fiero 88
figlio 10
figliolo 56
figliuolo 56
figura 15
fila 81
filo 47
filosofia 54
filosofo 54
finalmente 35
finchè 52
fine 25
finestra 32
finire 14
finito 89
fino 12, 20
finora 57
fiore 27
fisico 88
fissare 32
fisso 69
fiume 37
folla 45
fondamentale 63
fondare 62
fondo 13
fonte 86
forma 17
formare 23
formazione 85
formula 88
fornire 73
forno 93
forse 6
forte 18
fortuna 21
forza 10
fotografia 89
fra 5

mare 9
margine 62
marito 17
marittimo 96
marmo 73
maschera 79
maschio 85
massa 62
massimo 26
materiale 50, 92
matrimonio 100
mattina 26
mattino 65
maturo 91
me 9
medesimo 42
medio 62
mediterraneo 44
meglio 17
membro 76
memoria 27
meno 18, 22
mente 32
mentre 9, 20
meraviglia 80
meravigliare 89
meraviglioso 56
mercato 65
meritare 52
merito 61
mese 12
messa 81
mestiere 70
metà 25
metallico 88
metodo 49
metro 57
mettere 6
mezzo 21, 26
mezzogiorno 68
mi 5
migliaia 93
migliaio 93
miglio 87
migliore 27
milione 50
militare 63

mille 69
minimo 64
ministero 85
ministro 37
minore 47
minuto 34
mio 3
miracolo 75
miseria 80
missione 90
misterioso 81
mistero 57
misura 22
misurare 52
moda 83
modello 76
moderno 24
modesto 57
modo 5
moglie 20
molto 7, 26
momento 9
mondo 8
monte 33
monumento 65
morale 48
morire 13
mortale 93
morte 12
morto 66
mostrare 14
motivo 36
moto 58
movimento 30
muovere 24
muro 22
musica 35
mutare 35

nascere 13
nascondere 34
naso 75
natura 21
naturale 23
naturalmente 31

nave 55
nazionale 20
nazione 30
ne 3
nè 8
neanche 68
nebbia 55
necessario 17
necessità 22
negare 59
nemico 31
nemmeno 40
neppure 35
nero 21
nervoso 65
nessuno 14, 18
netto 86
neve 96
nido 83
niente 41
no 15
nobile 48
noi 5
nome 8
nominare 66
non 1
nonché 85
nord 59
norma 90
normale 93
nostro 4
nota 37
notare 19
notevole 40
notizia 20
noto 41
notte 10
novembre 81
novità 87
nudo 62
nulla 9
numero 19
numeroso 23
nuovo 5, 59
nuvola 94
nuvolo 94

ragione 13
rammentare 86
ramo 44
rapidamente 74
rapido 45
rappresentare 12
raro 51
reale 52
realmente 96
realtà 32
recare 29
recente 31
recentemente 94
reciproco 98
reggere 97
regina 98
regione 66
regno 66
regola 71
regolare 84, 96
relativo 67
relazione 29
religione 95
religioso 39
rendere 11
reparto 100
repubblica 61
resistenza 67
resistere 80
respingere 83
respiro 73
responsabile 72
restare 13
resto 17
rete 66
retta 85
ricchezza 48
ricco 16
ricerca 53
ricevere 22
richiamare 47
richiamo 81
richiedere 78
richiesta 84
ricominciare 96
riconoscere 12
ricordo 24

ridere 25
ridurre 41
riempiere 63
riempire 63
rifare 90
riferire 27
riflettere 46
rigido 79
riguardare 28
riguardo 48
rilevare 53
rilievo 67
rimanere 7
rimettere 58
ringraziare 65
rinnovare 80
ripartire 87
ripetere 19
riportare 44
riposo 75
riprendere 25
risalire 87
risolvere 42
rispetto 60
rispondere 16
risposta 54
risultare 50
risultato 42
ritenere 43
ritmo 61
ritornare 19
ritorno 33
ritratto 78
ritrovare 29
riudire 48
riuscire 10
riva 81
rivedere 62
rivelare 45
rivista 81
rivolgere 34
rivoluzione 67
robusto 100
rocce 99
roccia 99
romano 25
romanzo 80

rompere 62
rosa 71
rosso 30
rota 71
rovesciare 88
rubare 94
rumore 79
ruota 71

sacco 99
sacrificio 82
sacro 32
sala 21
sale 63
salire 15
saltare 95
salutare 34
salute 85
saluto 48
salvare 36
sangue 17
sano 60
santo 29, 83
sapere 4
sasso 90
scala 43
scambiare 74
scambio 71
scandalo 90
scarpa 87
scarso 73
scegliere 41
scena 26
scendere 26
scientifico 49
scienza 31
sciogliere 72
scomparire 58
scopo 25
scoppiare 61
scoprire 30
scorgere 85
scorrere 86
scorso 55
scritto 87

unito 76
università 40
universitario 91
uno 1, 6
uomini 4
uomo 4
usare 31
uscire 9
uso 41
utile41

vago 78
valere 20
valle 61
valore 14
vano 100
vario 14
vaso 95
vasto 27
ve 161
vecchio 8, 65
vedere 3
velo 77
velocità 78
vendere 56
venire 3
venti 47

vento 15
veramente 20
verde 37
vergogna 84
verità 18
vero 7
verso 9, 93
veste 59
vestire 64
vestito 76, 82
vetro 92
vi 8, 17
via 8, 22
viaggiatore 75
viaggio 18
vicenda 77
vicinanza 98
vicino 29, 40
villa 31
villaggio 93
vincere 44
vino 58
violento 68
violenza 95
virtù 45
visione 88
visita 53
visitare 50
viso 38

vista 22
vita 5
vittima 67
vittoria 54
vivere 10
vivo 13
vizio 89
voce 13
voglia 85
voi 18
volare 70
volentieri 86
volere 3
volgere 53
volo 77
volontà 24
volta 4
voltare 84
volto 35
volume 38
vostro 19
vuoto 56, 76

zio 77
zona 38

English Index

a 1
abandon 33
abandonment 84
able, be 2, 87
about 20
above 11
above all 33
absence 100
absolute 46
absolutely 60, 62
absorb 100
abundant 39
accept 27, 37
accident 83
accompany 16
accost 72
account 16
accurate 29
accuse 80
accustomed, be 69
achieve 16
acknowledge 80
acquaintance 36
acquainted 10
acquire 54
across 17
act 56, 66
action 9, 15
activity 31
acute 61
add 26
address 79
address (a letter) 77
administration 88
admiration 83
admire 62
admit 36
adopt 92
advance 65
adventure 99
advice 24
advisable 50
advise 74

aeroplane 99
afar 61
affair 34
affect 96
affection 67
affirm 46
after 4, 5
afternoon 68
afterwards 4, 5, 12
again 72
against 8
age 22
agent 82
agree 65
agreement 26
ah! 42
aid 48
air 11
alight 26
all 2, 3, 21
allow 6
almost 9, 19
alone 7
along 69
already 4
also 2, 97
always 4
amazement 83
American 85
among 5
amorous 98
amount 43
ample 39
amuse 87
an 1
ancient 14
and 1
and yet 51
angle 38
animal 36
anxiety 91
any 7
apparatus 99

appear 7, 11, 84
appearance 22, 99
argument 26
arm 18, 46
arms 46
army 55
around 12, 43, 97
arouse 72
arrange 31, 46
arrest 66
arrival 63
arrive 9, 13, 60
art 16
article 79
artist 40
artistic 55
as 2, 4, 92
ascend 15
ascertain 81
as far as 59
ask 12, 21, 36
as many 72
as much 72
assert 46
assign 82
assure 29
as yet 57
at least 16
atmosphere 55
attach 60
attack 60, 73
attempt 22, 73, 79
attend 25
attention 36, 85
attitude 79
August 76
authenticate 81
author 22
authority 68
average 62
avoid 38
awake 99
away 22

115

charming 64, 78
chat 70
chest 63
child 53
choose 41
chorus 90
Christian 48
church 16
cinema 79
circle 39, 86
circulate 48
circumstance 64
cite 76
citizen 70
city 8
civil 52
civil engineer 60
civilisation 43
clarify 74
class 43
classic(al) 55
clean 86
clear 14, 86
clever 87
climb 15
clock 74
close 14, 19
close by 40, 91
closed 28
cloud 94
coast 76
coat 42
coffee 62
cold 35, 79
collaboration 100
colleague 80
collect 17
collection 84
college 75
colonel 75
colonial 77
colour 19
column 72
come 3
comedy 45
comfort 44
comfortable 85

command 11, 55
commander 52
commerce 53
commercial 83
commission 51
commit 78
committee 83
common 19
commotion 84
communicate 50
communication 68
companion (female) 94
companion (male) 45
company 53
comparison 71
complete 15, 54
completely 47
complex 87, 89
complicated 73
compose 45
concede 31
concept 33
conception 61
concern 28
conclude 44
conclusion 52
condemn 82
condition 15
conduct 14, 47
conference 86
confess 63
confidence 69
confirm 48
confront 82
congenial 87
congress 84
connect 74
conquer 44, 93
conquest 52
conscience 54
consequence 45
consider 20
consideration 50
consist of 74
constant 95
constitute 19
constitution 51

constrain 56
construct 38
construction 51
consume 89
contact 54
contain 33
contemporary 58
contents 84
continent 82
continually 94
continue 11, 67, 78
continuous 44
continuously 94
contrary 94
contrary, on the 10
contrast 67
contribute 75
contribution 82
control 17, 23
convenient 39
conversation 69
convince 70
cool 38
corn 71
corner 38
corpse 60
correct 29
correspond 31
cost 76
costume 64
council 24
count (title) 67
count 43
country 29
country, native 39
country-house 31
countryman 51
countryside 29
couple 57
courage 14, 48, 75
course 24
courtyard 74, 94
cover 43, 66
covered 96
create 23
creation 85
creature 45

118

duke 65
during 13, 34
dust 86
duty 31, 57

earlier 9
early 30
earth 9
easily 63
east 70
eastern 73
easy 29
eat 32
echo 98
economic 37
economics 80
economy 80
edge 62, 95
education 59
effect 26
effort 38
eight 60
elapse 86
electric 59
elegance 94
elegant 79
element 23
embrace 56
emotion 84
emperor 62
empire 77
employ 92
employment 80
empty 56
encourage 97
end 13, 25, 33
endure 97
enemy 31
energy 49
English 36
engraving 53
enjoy 56
enormous 42
enough 27
enquiry 53, 63

enter 10
enterprise 72
entertain 87
entirely 46
entrance 73
entrust 50, 71
epoch 22, 48
equal 45, 92
erratic 78
error 41
escape 54, 90
especially 18, 79
essential 93
essentially 91
establish 40
et cetera 33
eternal 64
European 69
evening 12
event 10, 50, 77
ever 7
ever- 78
every 2, 3
everyone 45, 51
evident 68
evidently 73
evil 28
exact 51
exalt 85
examination 32, 55
examine 72
example 16
excellence 49
excellency 49
except 22
exception 100
exceptional 91
excite 55, 96
exclude 75
execute 63
exercise 70, 96
exhaust 96
exhibit 42
exhibition 70
exist 13
existence 42
expect 14, 74

expectation 66
expense 70
experience 30, 40, 65
experiment 97
explain 29, 74
explanation 86
explode 61, 96
expose 42
express 33
expression 25
extend 86
exterior 79
extol 85
extraordinary 25
extravagant 77
extreme 42
eye 8

face 19, 35, 38, 82
fact 9, 83
fact, in 18
factory 83
faith 24
faithful 76
fall 15
false 57
fame 85
family 12
famous 51
fancy 49
far 15
fascist 97
fashion 83
fat 23
fate 37
father 9
fatigue 46
fault 49
favour 72
fear 40, 89
February 90
feel 10
feeling 28
female 89, 94
festival 26

haste 95
hasten 69
hat 68
hate 86
hatred 82
have to 2
having 1
he 5, 6, 34
he who 34
head 11, 16
health 85
healthy 60
hear 26
hear again 48
heart 10
heat 92
heaven 14
heavenly 99
heavy 16
height 39, 57
help 46
henceforth 16
her 2, 11
her own 70
here 8, 30
here is (are) 23, 24
hero 68
herself 6, 81
hide 34
high 8
higher 26
hill 90
him 5
himself 6, 81
hinder 32
his 2
his own 70
historic 37
history 31
hitherto 57
hold 7
hold back 43, 70
holiday 26
hollow 70
holy 29, 32
homage 93
homework 57

honour 24
honourable 100
hope 31, 41
horizon 60
horse 37
hospital 71
host 58
hotel 43
hour 5
house 6
how 16
how many 34
how much 16, 21, 34
humanity 44
humble 57, 65
humid 74
humour 94
hundred 48, 80
hunger 94
hunt 78, 93
hunting 93
hurl down 69
husband 17
hypothesis 63

I 4
idea 11
if 4
ill 89
illness 28
illusion 60
illustrate 99
illustrious 46
image 40
imagination 49
imagine 34
immediate 49
immediately 80
immense 40
import 49
importance 19
important 30, 49
impose 39
impossible 55
impression 30

in 1
inclination 52
increase 53, 84
indeed 4
independence 71
independent 75
indicate 42, 44, 85
indication 94
indispensable 86
indistinct 78
individual 57, 97
induce 41
industrial 63
industry 39
inferior 85
infinite 46
influence 50
influenza 50
inform 23, 83
information 85
inhabit 58
initiative 64
injury 87
inner 76
innocent 94
in order that 3
in short 70
inside 31
inspire 83
instant 59
instead 10, 89
instinct 64
institute 21
instruct 23
instrument 67
insufficient 73
insure 29
intelligence 77
intelligent 58
intense 62
intention 32, 49
interest 19, 36, 44
interesting 28
interior 76
international 57
intimate 44
introduce 83

122

marble 73
margin 62
maritime 96
mark 35
market 65
marquis 93
marriage 100
marry 60
marvel 80, 89
marvellous 56
mask 79
Mass 81
mass 61
master 36, 47
material 50, 92
May 47
maybe 91
me 5, 9
meadow 75
mean 14, 69
meaning 37
means 21
meanwhile 31
measure 22, 52
measurement 22
meat 37
Mediterranean 44
meet 19
member 76
memory 24, 27
men 4
mention 72
merit 52, 61
merry 71
metallic 88
method 49
metre 57
midday 68
middle 26, 62
mile 87
military 63
milk 56
millet 87
million 50
mind 32, 48
minister 37, 80
ministry 85

minor 47
minute 34
miracle 75
mirror 57
misery 80
Miss 46
miss 16, 54
mission 19
mist 55
Mr 16
Mrs 19
model 76
modem 24
modest 57
moment 9, 20, 74
money 55
month 12
monument 65
moon 45
moral 48
more 2
moreover 56
morning 26, 65
morning, this 77
mortal 93
most, the 3
mother 12, 36
motion 58
motionless 74
motor-car 24, 33
mountain 33, 53
mouth 24
move 24
movement 30, 58
much 7
much, too 30
much, very 27
music 35
must 2
my 3
mysterious 81
mystery 57

naked 62
name 8, 66

narrow 38
nasty 47
nation 30
national 20
native country 39
natural 23
naturally 31
nature 21
naughty 46
near 13, 29, 32
neat 8
necessary 11, 17
neck 44
need 11, 19, 22
neighbourhood 98
neither 8
nervous 65
nest 83
net(work) 66
nevertheless 32
new 5, 59
news 20
newspaper 28
next 12, 16, 66
nice 87
night 10
no 7, 15, 18
noble 49
nobody 14, 47
noise 79
nominate 66
none 14
no-one 14, 47
nor 8
normal 90, 93
north 59
nose 75
not 1, 26
notable 40
not at all 41
note 19, 35, 37
not even 35, 40, 68
nothing 9
notice 20
noun 8
novel 80
novelty 87

political 19
politics 41
poor 32
poor man 71
pope 91
position 21, 23
positive 88
possess 35
possibility 24
possible 15
pot 95
powder 86
power 10, 22, 59
powerful 49
practical 30
pray 36
prayer 68
precaution 85
precede 49
preceding 65
precious 53
precise 28
precisely 41, 54
prefer 44
première 100
preparation 89
prepare 20
presence 32
present 11, 23
preserve 38
president 77
press 53, 56, 98
price 82
pride 78
primitive 79
prince 30
principle 35, 41
prison 88
prisoner 95
private 33, 81
probably 55
problem 17
proceed 43, 73
process 59
produce 29, 44, 63
product 63
production 49

professor 14
programme 58
progress 54
project 74
promise 78, 79
promote 99
pronounce 60
proof 32
proper 8
property 47
propose 24
proprietor 74
protagonist 92
protection 53
proud 88
provide 46
provide with 73
province 65
provisional 96
provoke 61, 96
public 33, 41
publication 74
publish 27
pull 21, 62
pull off 81
punishment 29
pure 32
purpose 25
pursue 67
push 30
put 6, 24
put forward 65
put on 64
put out 58

quality 46
quantity 64
quarter 89
queen 98
quench 58
question 29, 41
quick 36, 45
quicken 92
quickly 30
quite 60

race 78
radio 79
railing 95
rain 63, 91
raise 33, 34, 44, 67
rapidly 74
rare 51
rather 10, 33
ray 61
reach 9, 16
read 17
reader 76
ready 36
real 7, 52, 58
real estate 74
reality 32
really 20, 27, 96
reason 13
rebuild 90
recall 47, 81, 86
receive 37
recent 31
recently 94
reciprocal 98
reckon 43
recognise 12
recommend 71
recover 25, 29
red 30
reduce 41, 84, 91
re-enter 66
refer 27
refined 88
reflect 46
regard 48
region 60
regular 96
rehearse 40
reign 66
relation 24, 29
relative 67
relief 67
relieve 37
religion 95
religious 39
remain 7
remind 86

sign 15
silence 30
silent 28, 92
silk 84
silver 55
similar 23
simple 18
simply 91
sin 48
since 60, 62, 92
sincere 92
sing 36
single 83
singular 48
sir 16
sister 47
sit 33
site 42
situation 36
six 59
size 60
sky 14
sky blue 99
sleep 35, 89
slow 66
slowly 69, 77
small 1
smaller 47
smell 72
smile 47, 68
smoke 90
snow 96
so 4, 13
social 41
society 21
soft 51
soil 68
soldier 44
solemn 72
solid 91
solution 51
some 5, 97
somebody 33, 47
someone 33, 47
something 39
sometimes 88
so much 20

son 10
song 41
sore 61
sorrow 29
soul 12
sound 47, 54
source 86
south 51, 68
souvenir 24
space 69
speak 5
special 28
species 17
speech 20
speed 78
spend 90
spirit 15
spiritual 62
sport 40
spread 36, 51, 87
square 28, 43
stage 26
stamp 53
stand 3
standpoint 22
star 34
start again 96
state 14, 56
stated 80
stately 84
station 27
statue 85
stay 3, 13
steady 21, 26
steal 94
step 27
still 4, 32, 72
stir 99
stone 90
stop 19, 66, 94
story 88
straight line 85
strange 35
stream 65
street 8, 14
strength 10
stretch (out) 36

strict 38
strike 66
string 80
stroll 26
strong 18
struggle 39
study 17, 30
style 86
subject 26, 50
substance 56
substitute 63
subtle 31
succeed 10, 36
success 38
such 9, 23
such a one 37
sudden 43, 96
suddenly 9, 91
suffer 37, 68
suffice 17
sufficient 61
sufficiently 95
suffocate 88
suggest 83
suit 39, 76
Summer 53
summons 81
sun 13
Sunday 74
superior 26
support 97
suppose 73
supreme 26
sure 7, 21
surface 81
surprise 78, 100
surround 95
surroundings 61
suspect 67
suspicion 67
sustain 36
sweet 35
symbol 81
sympathy 99
system 28

vain 100
valley 61
value 14
van 82
various 12, 14
vase 95
vast 27
vault 98
veil 77
verse 93
very 7, 21, 26, 29
very much 59
vice 89
victim 67
victory 54
view 22
vigorous 49
villa 31
village 11, 93
violence 95
violent 68
virtue 45
vision 88
visit 50, 53
voice 13
void 76
volume 38

wait 14, 25
waitress 78
waiving 84
wake (ship's) 97
wake up 72
walk 41
wall 22, 46
want 3
war 9
warn 23
wash 98
water 10

wave 54
way 8, 14, 37, 57
we 5
weak 97
wealth 48
wear 6
wear out 89
weather 5
wedding 100
week 35
weep 46
weight 33
welfare 85
well 7, 16
western 96
wet 74
whatever 56, 82
wheel 71
when 4
whence 76
where 5, 35
whereas 9
whether 4
which 3, 13, 76
whichever 56
while 9, 52
white 24
white man 99
whiteness 99
who 1, 13
whoever 7, 13
whole 5, 32
whom 4, 7
wide 23
wife 20
will 24
willing 3
willingly 86
win 44
wind 15, 87
window 32
wine 58

wing 51
Winter 36
wire 47
wish 3, 35, 85
wit 15
with 1
within 5, 31, 34, 39
without 3
witness 48
woe 88
woman 8, 89
wood 61, 69
word 7
work 7, 10, 23, 46
worker 79
worse 86
worth 20
worthy 48
wound 66
write 11
writer 50
writing 87
wrongly 57

year 3
yes 15
yesterday 39
yet 4, 6
yield 11, 91
you 7, 8, 18, 21, 61
young 19
young lady 46
young people 90
your 90, 20
youth 90

zone 38

129

BOOKS FROM OLEANDER

FRENCH KEY WORDS
Xavier-Yves Escande

BULGARIA: A TRAVEL GUIDE
Philip Ward

BEFRIENDING: A SOCIOLOGICAL CASE-HISTORY
Michèle Hagard and Vic Blickem

WESTERN INDIA: A TRAVEL GUIDE
Philip Ward

FRIULAN: LANGUAGE AND LITERATURE
D.B. Gregor

LOST SONGS: NEW POEMS
Philip Ward

RAIN FOLLOWING: NEW POEMS
Sue Lenier

THE LIFE AND MURDER OF HENRY MORSHEAD
Ian Morshead

ROMAGNOL: LANGUAGE AND LITERATURE
D.B. Gregor

SOUTH INDIA: A TRAVEL GUIDE
Philip Ward

THE LAND OF MIDIAN
Sir Richard Burton

ARABIAN GULF INTELLIGENCE
comp. R.H. Thomas

FORGOTTEN GAMES: A NOVEL
Philip Ward

FATHER GANDER'S NURSERY RHYMES
Per Gander

THE AEOLIAN ISLANDS
Philip Ward

FROM THE LION ROCK & THE SEA VOYAGE
Carey Harrison

A DICTIONARY OF COMMON FALLACIES
Philip Ward